C000183824

Cutting around Cambridgeshire

KINDERSLEY INSCRIPTIONS
IN THE COUNTY

Lida Lopes Cardozo Kindersley

AND

Thomas Sherwood

CARDOZO KINDERSLEY · CAMBRIDGE 2012

A slate intended for
Anglesey Abbey.

HAE TILIAE TOMENTOSAE
IN MEMORIAM
HVITLESTONI BROVGHTON
PRIMI BARONIS FAIRHAVEN
DESIGNATORIS HORTORVM
ABBATIAE ANGLESEIANAE
QVI OBIIT ABHINC ANNOS C
POSITAE SVNT
ANNO DOMINI MCMXCVI

First published 2012

Designed by Phil Treble, using the series layout designed by Eiichi Kono.

Photographs by Philip Moore and from the Cardozo Kindersley Archives.

Maps drawn by Fiona Boyd.

The book has been set in 12 pt Emilida, a typeface designed by Lida Lopes Cardozo Kindersley, digitised by ITA Kono Design, commissioned by Timothy Guy Design for EMI. The typeface was enhanced in 2010, with many OpenType features and attention to spacing, by Eben Sorkin.

Printed in the United Kingdom at the University Press, Cambridge

ISBN-13: 978-1-107-62242-5 paperback

Copies available from:
Cambridge University Press Bookshop
1 Trinity Street
Cambridge CB2 1SZ
UK

Frontispiece: Congregational Schoolroom, Royston (page 18).

Contents

Introduction

Having been 'Cutting through the Colleges' and 'Cutting across Cambridge' (Cambridge University Press 2010 & 2011), it is high time we cut our way around the county. Our work is all over the world, but Cambridgeshire has always been a first for the Workshop.

As in the City book, we can present only a selection of what has been done in the county for over half a century: there is just too much, in a body of commissions that is always on the go. Church and civic work is side by side as before. We open with two special chapters; then go to the outskirts of Cambridge, and spiral round clockwise through the region. We end in Ely Cathedral. Strict county boundaries have been crossed on occasion in order to include conveniently grouped sites.

We were pleased to find the great bulk of what we were looking for: less of the lost property that has exercised us before. The threesome of these books underline what engages us most of all – that letters cut in stone and other materials are part of the fabric of human experience, to be held very close. Or else we die.

1945 in Barton

David Kindersley (1915–95) had been Eric Gill's apprentice 1934–36 before setting out on on his own in Sussex and Dorset. Gill's widow asked him back in 1943 to take over (rescue the more accurate term) that master's workshop in High

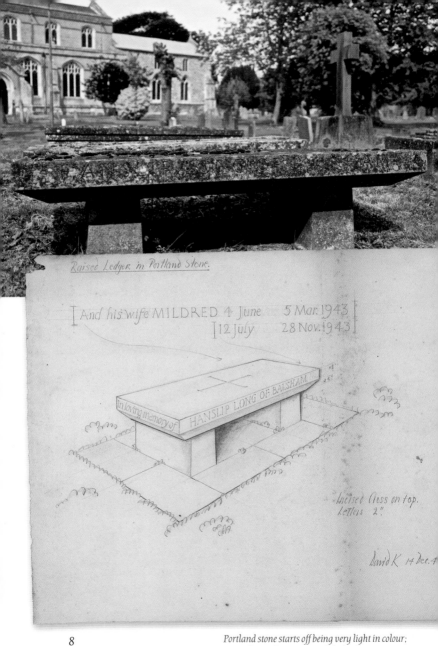

Raised Ledger in Portland Stone.

[And his wife MILDRED 4 June   5 Mar. 1943]
              [12 July   28 Nov. 1943]

In loving memory of   HANSLIP LONG OF BALSHAM

Incised Cross on top.
Letters 2".

David K 14 Dec. 4

8

Portland stone starts off being very light in colour;
it weathers to become part of the landscape.

Wycombe, Buckinghamshire. David then moved to Barton in January 1945 in order to set up his own new workshop. It was a risky venture, particularly with two apprentices also engaged – would the commissions come in those austere post-war times? The Cambridge University Printer Brooke Crutchley had been encouraging, and there was an immediate January commission for a large memorial cross in a Cambridge cemetery (Lendon Smith 1946, see 'Cutting across Cambridge', Cambridge University Press 2011).

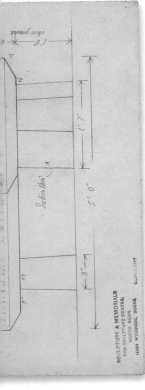

It must have been specially pleasing that two further commissions arose at once in the village of Barton: Hopton Wood stones for Elliott Howes at The Five Houses, the first of 7 commissions there (see Barton page 34). They were followed by another big 1945 piece, a Portland stone ledger for Balsham churchyard – In loving memory of HANSLIP LONG OF BALSHAM and his wife MILDRED. Six other requests for stones in various counties also rolled in; a good beginning after all. The Workshop, with David 30 years old, was en route, moving later to the old school house at 152 Victoria Road, where it remains. We describe the Cambridgeshire harvest of the first 65 years.

On the making of a slate roundel

The to & fro between this book's designer and
lettercutter is always a nice mix of pleasure and
business. Phil thought of a table with a large central
recess for a stone by Lida, and they talked about it.
Simon Rickles, a cabinet-maker in Leeds and an old
school friend of Phil's, was asked to design and make
the oak table, and then the uncut slate went to him so
that the piece could be given the right snug recess.
The finished table arrived in East Cambridgeshire;
and the stone back in the Workshop. These pages
picture the rest of its story, from drawing out to
cutting, painting and gilding. And finally fitting:
tricky, because the wood had naturally changed
shape during a 4 months' wait.

   The design of the unusual alphabet that resulted
for this 2011 Welsh slate is based on David
Kindersley's 1967 experiments; such tapered
letters are also seen in the Keatley collection's
MOVE A STONE (see page 25). David
originally wrote of this 'reed' alphabet as 'Roman
capitals envisaged in oriental terms'.

*The start: lunchtime
discussion on how the
inscription for this
special table might
work. What kind of
lettering for an
alphabet that will be
seen all day and night?*

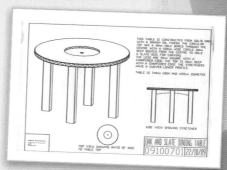

The usual first step following discussion with the client is the preparation of a scale drawing. Here, knowing the physical constraints for the design, we went straight into drawing onto the slate.

No initial scale design – drawing out onto the stone begins, and then the cutting – that took 6 weeks. We make a rubbing of the finished piece for our records, and wash the dust out of the letters. And the apostrophe is gilded.

We arrive with the slate, and have to fit it – the sides have to be rubbed down for this, because the wood of the table has now moved. There is an unveiling, and the first alphabet lunch.

13

Lida cutting in Orwell

The Workshop, November 2011

The Keatley collection

'To commission an inscription is a token of personal and public commitment' wrote David McKitterick in 'Cutting through the Colleges' (Cambridge University Press 2010). And a thrilling experience for client and lettercutter, we might add. A return of that client to the Workshop for a second commission is new delight. An enthusiast going for his thirtieth Kindersley piece seems perhaps unlikely, but is the subject of this chapter.

This remarkable collection is catalogued at the end of the book. We begin with 9 stones to be seen in Royston, just outside the southern border of the county.

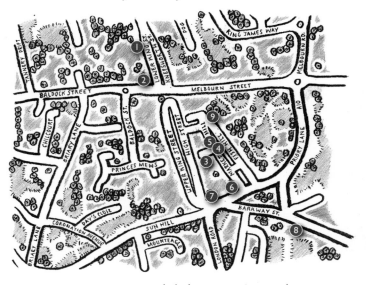

1. *Congregational Schoolroom*
2. *Kiln House*
3. *Henry Andrews*
4. *Tey House*
5. *Royston National School*
6. *Corn Exchange*
7. *REFECIT MCMLXXV*
8. *Wheelwrights*
9. *1891 SD*

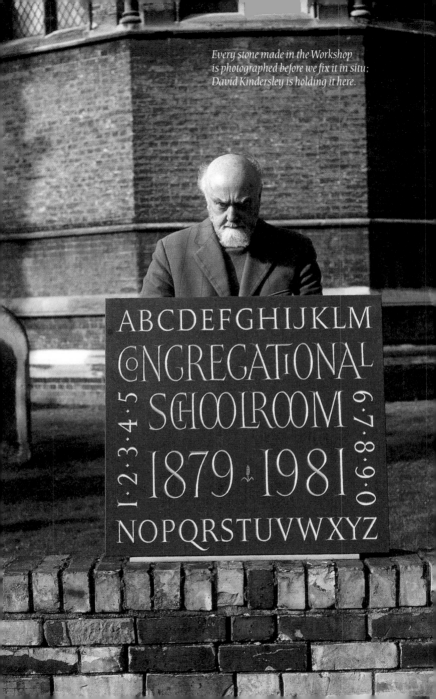

Every stone made in the Workshop
is photographed before we fix it in situ:
David Kindersley is holding it here.

Royston

The museum in Lower King Street,
a limb of Kneesworth Street at its
southern end, has a 1983 Welsh
slate CONGREGATIONAL
SCHOOLROOM high up on its front.
Round the corner from there, right into
Baldock Street and then Kiln House
Yard, is KILN HOUSE, a Welsh
slate naming it in 1989.

Walking south into the High Street,
turn left into George Lane for HENRY
ANDREWS at number 1: a 1979
Welsh slate roundel commemorating
the 'Astronomer, Mathematician
& Author of Moore's Almanack'.
TEY HOUSE (1990 Welsh slate)
is just beyond, across Market
Hill; this is inside
and can be spied
through the
glass front.

The slate has been let into the
brickwork, rather than being fixed
on top. This gives more protection.

The Royston
townscape has
been enriched
by its many
Keatley stones
– the passer-by is
enlightened as well
as charmed.

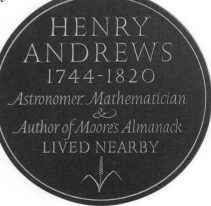

18

A little down Market Hill, facing west, is ROYSTON NATIONAL SCHOOL, a 1981 Welsh slate high up. Then near the top of Market Hill is the ROYSTON CORN EXCHANGE, a triangular Welsh slate above its entrance gate (1989).

Looking west across the square from here, the house left of the Bull Inn has a round Welsh slate (1977) above a shop: REFECIT MCMLXXV, commemorating that restoration.

The Royston crow being shaped onto slate.

Turning left (east) out of Market Hill round the Corn Exchange, it is a short walk to a busy traffic junction, and then right (south) to a building near the bottom of Barkway Street. Facing north, WHEELWRIGHTS 1997 is a circular 1998 Welsh slate high up under the roof, with an ear of wheat as characteristic recurring Keatley signature; it marks the site of a former Wheelwrights' Shop.

On the way back to the start of the tour, turn down Fish Hill. At the bottom the last house on the right (east) bears another Welsh slate with ears of wheat (1980). It says 1891 SD surrounded by *REFECIT MCMLXXIX*: the complete history for the restoration of Lady Sidney Dacre's rooms.

A variety of designs for John Keatley's buildings: we work together at this.

Private collection
A 1969 diamond Welsh slate
of an alphabet, with that date
below, begins the long association
with the Workshop. Two other alphabets
on Welsh slates, contrasting flourished
and wild calligraphic styles, are from 1983 and
1990. For really exuberant flourishes there is a 1986 Welsh slate
alphabet with I J K as central feature. An italic alphabet cut in
1977 is on a glass disc.

Over the years, the Workshop
has made many alphabets for
this collection. The one on the
right starts with A on the left;
I J K move down vertically,
and the continuation is
anti-clockwise.

The Workshop does not carry out other people's designs, but relented on this principle in 1999, for the vibrant American calligrapher Arthur Baker. His alphabet is now on a Welsh slate, and the work posed a challenging task. The lettercutter's art had to be matched with the different techniques and toolkit of calligraphy. It demanded quite unusual practices for the Workshop, for instance tracing an enlarged paper copy of the alphabet onto the stone. What works on paper is not the same for slate; much was learned.

The opening of LAKE HOUSE is celebrated on a strikingly elongated diamond, a Welsh slate of 1999, once in Royston.

IN MEMORY OF
JAMES WALTER STANLEY
KEATLEY
OF ROYSTON · HERTFORDSHIRE
1904 - 1978
AND OF HIS WIFE
HELEN RANKIN THOMPSON
1901 - 1997

A coat of arms painted and gilded in full heraldic colours. Bead moulding all around gives it a soft edge.

From the same year a rectangular Portland stone memorial is for JAMES WALTER STANLEY KEATLEY and HIS WIFE HELEN RANKIN THOMPSON.

THE KEATLEY TRUST COLLECTION is a 1992 Welsh slate that includes flourishes, leaves, roses... The roses are red and white for the family's long ties with both Lancashire and Yorkshire.

The lettering has since been cut off: it was carved during the late rush of a TV studio recording, not in Workshop conditions.

An interesting acquisition for the collection dates from 1952: a relief of the BBC coat of arms on a Welsh slate. Originally it had 'Nation shall speak peace unto Nation' below; David Kindersley demonstrated cutting these letters live on television that year.

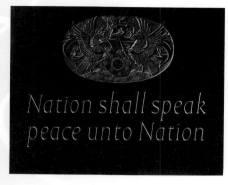

The collection includes highly individual compositions in stone, both witty and serious. Inscribed on a glass bowl is 'Because there is a word for it we imagine we know it' (1981). SPARE NOT BUT WASTE NOT is a 1984 Welsh slate for the attention of cooks. MOVE A STONE STIR A WING (2009 Welsh slate) began as a garden piece, inspired by Francis Thompson's poetry.

See pages 12 & 13 (Phil's table) for another example of 'reed' letters, with their weight on the inside or outside.

25

We always make a scale drawing (never a full-size one) to show whether we have understood the brief, and achieved the joint objective for the design.

10½"

CHOP
YOUR
OWN
WOOD

WARM
YOUR
SELF
TWICE

24" wide

Full size all letters

LIDA & JOHN – WELSH SLATE – PAINTED & GILDED SCHEME

Also aimed at gardeners is 'The labour we delight in physics pain' (from Macbeth), a 2009 Welsh slate. CHOP YOUR OWN WOOD AND WARM YOURSELF TWICE is a 2011 Welsh slate. And to exercise your ingenuity: solve the puzzle on the roundel of Welsh slate (2006)!

The labour we delight in physics pain

Forget-me-nots were carefully placed on the outer rim only: a dancing edge!

26

More still: there is an alabaster box inscribed *KK (2001)* and a wooden bowl with *ARABELLA HELEN... (1988)*. And a lovely much elongated rectangle that bears the family crest at its far right, after *ABSTINVI LIBRIS IVVENIS...*, a 1986 Welsh slate. The elegant Latin is roughly about liking horses more than books when young – and now turning the stables into a library.

So: a treasure house. The full list for this collection shows the additional work that is outside the county.

Keatley commissions are ever challenging, pushing us to unusual solutions. The very sharp woodcarving tools needed are quite different from those for stonework.

Outer Cambridge

Barton

Before you get to the village after leaving Cambridge, just across the motorway, there is a very quiet burial ground on the left: St Mark's, of which the Newnham church in Cambridge is the parent. There are 5 headstones, quite different in designs and materials; the burly shape of the 1977 Horton stone for the composer MILA GERSHEVITCH contrasts with more slender slates and Ancaster stones – all names are listed at the back of the book.

The GERSHEVITCH stone was carefully shaped out of a massive rectangular block.

St Peter's church has a 1951 oak inscription above a door at its west end: *IN MEMORY OF RICHARD & MARIANNE HOLBEN*. Outside, on the north-western fringe of the churchyard, a cremation tablet is in the ground for *IDA EDWARDS & HAROLD EDWARDS* (2001 Welsh slate).

Heading west and then south from the church into High Street, towards the A603, the village's recreation ground appears on the right. The children's playground sports a disused wooden hut, and in front of it there is a 1953 Welsh slate roundel set into a Hopton Wood stone square. The slate has a compass surrounded by 11 place names adjacent to the village; on the square *THE CHILDRENS CORNER & THE TREES WERE SET OUT TO COMMEMORATE THE CORONATION OF HER MAJESTY QUEEN ELIZABETH II*, with 1953 having a figure in each corner. This is a charmer.

The Hopton Wood stone surround sets off the central slate roundel.

Dales
Barn

Back in the centre of the village by the pond, on the small
traffic island of green, there is a triangular concrete pillar with
6 inlaid aluminium panels of 1977. THE QUEEN'S SILVER
JUBILEE 1977 is the threefold upper circular inscription, with
BARTON, tun and sheaves below. Opposite the pond, DALES
BARN, a 1988 slate on the house marks David Kindersley's first
workshop in the county.

Dales Barn was the start of David Kindersley's Workshop
in Cambridgeshire (see Introduction page 7)

DESIGN BARTON

A 1971 Welsh slate also marks another
house in the village: 'Towns End'.

Just before leaving the village by
the Comberton Road, a remarkable set
of low buildings appears on the left: The Six Houses. These are
now the homes of retired professional gardeners run by Perennial
(formerly the Gardeners' Royal Benevolent Society); during
WWII these began as
The Five Houses (Almshouses). They contain 6 Kindersley
stones – a further oak gate inscription for Five Houses has
gone with the former name. With care and tact, visitors will
not be unwelcome for seeing these outside features of a fine and
touching development; but they must remember that these are
private homes, with private car parking!

We begin with a central small archway, set back to the left
after the entrance path: a 1945 Hopton Wood stone explains

These Cottages
were built by Elliott Howes
in memory of his five sisters
Alice Agnes Nellie
Hilda and Jessie
Here are their names but where is the memory

'These Cottages were built by Elliott Howes in memory of his five sisters Alice Agnes Nellie Hilda and Jessie Here are their names but where is the memory'. On either side of this block is poetry. The other 1945 Hopton Wood stone, south is 'Whither came I whither go I...'; north is 'From where to where who knows...' on a 1947 Delabole slate with Portland stone moulding. The Portland stone bench beneath has SIT HERE AWHILE AND THINK OF KINDLY THINGS (1947).

Different materials ring the changes for the stonework throughout these gardens.

Finally, the west of the block shows two Yellow Magnesian Mansfield limestone plaques either side of the doors there, with the portraits of the subjects in relief. That of 1947 was for ELLIOTT HOWES DESIGNER DONOR, and 1950 for E R HAZELDEN MASTER BUILDER.

The portraits in relief are remarkable; David Kindersley had a fine eye for portraiture as shown on these roundels. Fortunately they are well protected under the eaves of the cottage.

See the comments already made on page 27 for the very sharp woodcarving tools needed here – not our usual kit! Being a woodland burial ground, no stonework is allowed.

This is all quite magical, on a very intimate scale amid beautiful gardens.

And once out of the village, immediately on the right there is a woodland burial place. Veer right after the wooden building and follow the arc-like walk, past one large bench till you come to a smaller rectangular oak one on the left, of 2007. *NICHOLAS THEODORE VENIZELOS TAPTIKLIS BELOVED HUSBAND OF BARBARA HOW I MISS YOUR LOVE* is inscribed on the seat with Hippocrates' snake as medical symbol. It is very still here; Barton is a tranquil place.

DONALD
ARTHUR
PRATER
OBE·DLitt
1918-2001
SOLDIER
DIPLOMAT
WRITER
BELOVED
HUSBAND OF
PATRICIA
1914-2005

Coton

St Peter's churchyard in this small village, just west of Cambridge across the motorway, has two interesting headstones. A Portland stone of 2003 for DONALD ARTHUR PRATER records the soldier, diplomat and writer, with his wife PATRICIA PRATER added in 2005. RITA HOWARD Midwife is a riven green slate (2007), with the back reading 'we come to God by love not by navigation'. A 2000 Welsh slate names LONG CLOSE, a private house in the village.

This green slate is a riven piece of rock in its natural state – contrast with the more formal shape for PRATER opposite.

Small commissions like this house name delight the Workshop: we love making cheerful additions to ordinary daily life.

Fen Ditton

The cemetery at the end of Church Street has two contrasting
headstones to the east. Right of the path is ALFRED WATERS,
a small Kirkstone green slate of 1990. And to the left PETER
ARUNDEL JEWELL on a larger Portland stone that also bears
foliage, a fox and cockerel... A private garden nearby fondly
records two dogs, JESS & JACK on a 2003 York stone.

The Portland stone, with
its Gill-inspired decorative
border, records a full life
– in contrast to the child's
'unwritten slate' nearby.

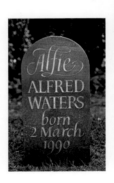

Fulbourn

Coming from Cambridge, Fulbourn
Hospital is on the left; its Elizabeth
House has a 2001 Welsh slate in the
entrance porch for the opening by
HRH THE PRINCE OF WALES.

THE REDEVELOPED
FULBOURN HOSPITAL
WAS OPENED BY
HRH
THE PRINCE OF WALES
ON 27 MARCH 2001

*Formal capital letters do not invite
flourishing, but italic capitals allow it.*

THOMAS H · SIMMS
1908 · 1990
HIS INSIGHT AND ENERGY
GUIDED THIS RESTORATION

*Lettering here is filled with
white enamel paint, making
it stand out even more as the
brass darkens with time.*

Onward on the road to the village, Fulbourn Windmill appears
on the right (with special openings) – a beam on the ground
floor bears a small brass plaque of 1992 for the man behind the
restoration THOMAS H. SIMMS.

In the village itself, the churchyard of St Vigor has a 2004 oval green slate in the ground for ROSEMARY CAROLYN TOWNLEY (bear right along the path). FULBOURN MANOR is adjacent to the church, the name cut into the pillars flanking the entrance (2004).

The cemetery is a little way south from here in Sanders Lane. To the right after the entrance is a wall of memorial tablets, with *WINDSOR IAN WEBSTER* (1994 Welsh slate). Further south on the right a tall headstone is for *NORA FLORENCE SALT* (2010 Brown York stone). It has Lincoln Cathedral in relief above, watching over a family with roots in Lincoln; the back is also inscribed.

WINDSOR IAN
WEBSTER
1926-1993
*A dear husband and
loving father*

The back of this stone quotes Shakespeare's Cymbeline.

Thou
thy worldly task
hast done,
Home art gone
and
ta'en thy wages

Nora Florence
SALT née Young
1919-2008
Wife of
Eric Douglas
Sydney SALT
1916-1999

Girton

*TRINITY FARM in
Huntingdon Road is a fine
1995 green slate fronting the
road; on leaving Cambridge it
is on the left before the Girton
College site. The Cambridge
University Farm, a little*

*further north, has 4 glass plaques naming the Agronomy Centre,
its benefactors and rooms (2007).*

   *In Girton village, opposite the church, a 1987 Kirkstone
green slate is for ALICE HIBBERT-WARE and her
memorial garden.*

   *In St Andrew's churchyard there are 4 headstones. DAVID
BERNARD EVANS, a 1998 Welsh slate, is on the right of
the entrance approach; the back celebrates 'A pioneer in renal
dialysis Physician & friend...'.*

*The back of a gravestone is
often unexplored.*

At the rear of the church are JEAN BUITER (Welsh slate 2006), JOANNA MARY HARTLEY (Welsh slate 1999) and MARGARET ROBSON (Portland stone 2004). They too have inscriptions on their backs.

To
see a World
in a Grain of Sand
And a Heaven
in a Wild Flower
Hold Infinity
in the palm
of your hand
And Eternity
in an hour

In loving memory

JOANNA
MARY
HARTLEY
2nd February 1938
10th July 1998

To every thing there is a season

JEAN
BUITER
1950-2005
Beloved mother of
David & Elizabeth

He who binds to
himself a joy
Does the winged
life destroy
But he
who kisses the joy
as it flies
Lives in eternity's
sunrise

In loving memory of
MARGARET
ROBSON
30th May 1935
30th March 2003

wife of JOHN
FREDERICK
ROBSON

The italic lettering was engraved straight into the oval brass plate.

City Crematorium (off the A14 Huntingdon Road)
A 1971 green bronze plaque for JUDITH MARIA
LAUTERPACHT hangs on a tree in the south-west corner of
the Memorial Rose Garden, just before the spinney is reached.

Grantchester
The churchyard of St Andrew & St
Mary has long associations with
Corpus Christi College. The 'pelican
in its piety' symbol of the college
was carved by David Kindersley
in 1950 as part of his 3 metre-high
Portland stone column, a memorial
to College Fellows. It stands behind
the 2006 green slate headstone for
MICHAEL McCRUM, a past
Master; both have already appeared
in our 'Cutting through the Colleges'
(Cambridge University Press 2010).

We illustrate here 6 of the Workshop's stones for individuals in the churchyard – names are listed at the end of the book.

DENNIS
NELIGAN
COLE
1921-2006

Irving Bamdas
FRITZ
SCIENTIST
1927-1960

CHARLES
BURFORD
GOODHART
ZOOLOGIST
1919-2000
AND HIS WIFE
DIANA
1920-2005
ADORED BY FAMILY
FRIEND TO ALL

John
Pennington
1912
1976

So many possibilities – we discuss each commission very carefully, in order to make exactly the right stone for the individual commemorated.

JOAN ELSA
DAY
1911-2004
Painter &
wife of
THOMAS DUNCAN
DAY
1907-1976
Pathologist

Sheila Anne
Rodwell OBE
1947-2009
Inspired scientist
and
loving wife
Adored & respected
by all

Behind the church (south) a Garden of Remembrance is dominated by a large Welsh slate with Portland stone capping REMEMBER BEFORE GOD THE SOULS OF THOSE WHOSE ASHES LIE BURIED HERE, from 1975. Further names were inscribed in 1978.

Byron's Pool is south-east of the village, approached by a pleasant short walk through woods, from a car park just east of the river. ROB WARD is a 2005 green slate memorial to be found on the left of the upper path, shortly before the pool is reached.

New inscriptions were added after 1978 by a former Workshop apprentice.

The chance encounter with this tranquil woodland piece: someone who loved the place.

Histon & Impington
The opening of BURDETT
HOUSE is recorded on a 1997
Welsh slate at the front of 58A
Station Road. The churchyard of St
Andrew's has a 2000 Portland stone
for JAMES LUKE MACAULAY,
just right of the entrance. The cemetery
is at the corner of Water Lane & Mill Lane,
with two headstones of a family celebrated at Impington
Village College below. On the eastern fringe a 1995 York
stone is for STEPHEN OSWALD CHIVERS, *his wife*
and their daughter; left of the entrance along the southern fringe
there is WILLIAM NOEL CHIVERS, *a 2002 green slate.*

Everything
in italics:
it makes for
a lively flow.

'Our son & brother' is
enveloped in the protective
swoop of the ampersand.

Here 'In loving memory'
is a radiant sunrise.

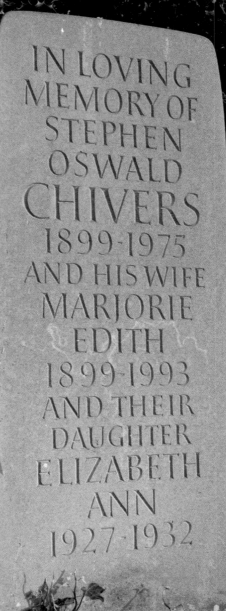

IN LOVING
MEMORY OF
STEPHEN
OSWALD
CHIVERS
1899-1975
AND HIS WIFE
MARJORIE
EDITH
1899-1993
AND THEIR
DAUGHTER
ELIZABETH
ANN
1927-1932

Note the unusual shape of this York stone.

IN 1939 THE DIRECTORS OF
CHIVERS & SONS LTD
PROVIDED THE ADULT WING
FOR RESIDENTS
IN THE PARISHES SERVED BY
IMPINGTON VILLAGE COLLEGE
THE GIFT COMPRISED THE
LIBRARY THE COMMON ROOM
THE LECTURE ROOM & VARIOUS
RECREATION ROOMS

GOLDEN JUBILEE
1939 🙰 1989
Keep the young
generation in hail
And bequeath them
no tumbled house.
REDEDICATION OF
IMPINGTON
VILLAGE COLLEGE
by
The Lord Lieutenant for the
County of Cambridgeshire
Mr MICHAEL BEVAN

IMPINGTON
VILLAGE COLLEGE

The disappearance of this nameboard is a pointer to wood being impermanent – it needs looking after.

IMPINGTON VILLAGE COLLEGE
was an oak nameboard from 1978,
no longer seen; the College also
has 3 Welsh slates. IN 1939 THE
DIRECTORS OF CHIVERS & SON
is in the Carnegie Room (1975), and
the main entrance hall has GOLDEN
JUBILEE (1989). THE SYLVIA
WEST LIBRARY (2001) is outside.

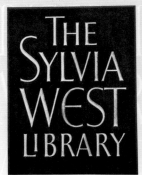

THE
SYLVIA
WEST
LIBRARY

*A memorial to an inspired head,
devoted to education.*

54

Madingley

AMERICAN CEMETERY
It began in 1943 as the temporary Cambridge
American Military Cemetery on land donated to
the United States by the University of Cambridge.
The formal dedication was in 1956, and it is the
only WWII American Cemetery in the country:
a moving and breathtaking place.

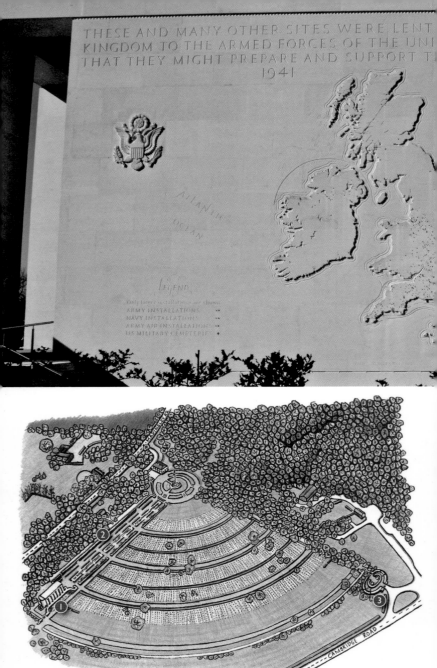

This huge map had the whole Workshop cutting, perched on scaffolding.

*The Visitors' Building & Chapel at the eastern end is of Portland
stone, and bears two gigantic relief maps – Britain with
northern France outside on the south wall, and the world inside.
The Workshop carried out this work between 1954 and 1960;
it was a quite massive task. The carving was done in situ.
The exterior map of Britain is remarkable in its meticulous
attention to every detail of the coastal outline; in the fine
American arms with eagle on the left, and the flourished Legend
below it.*

1. *Chapel*
2. *Tablets of the Missing*
3. *Cambridge Road Eagle*

Everything for the inside map was constructed by the Workshop:
the bronze lettering, the model aircraft, boats and other symbols,
the rods showing flight paths… David Kindersley's Workshop
is signed on the bottom left – a rare feature. Outside high above
the entrance there is a second example of the carved arms of the
United States.

OCHI RICHARD G · 2 LT · 413 BOMB SQ 96 BOMB GP(H)
ZANT PAT C · S SGT · 413 BOMB SQ 96 BOMB GP(H)
IAN JOSEPH H · 1 LT · 506 SQ 404 FTR BOMBER G
EL VICTOR L · · 1 LT · · 352 FTR SQ 353 FTR GP
GELBAUGH ROBERT H · T SGT · 535 BOMB SQ 381 BOMB GP
LRATH ELMER R · SGT · 326 BOMB SQ 92 BOMB GP(H
ORHEES HAROLD · CPL · · 306 QM BN · ·
ORHESS CHARLES R · 1 LT · HQ SQ 50 TRP CARR WG

✳ MEDAL OF HONOR

The Tablets of The Missing is a huge wall with over 5000 names. David Kindersley was approached about cutting these; but given the deadline for the task and the available manpower of the Workshop, had to decline. However, he did add a few names that came to light later, and these handcut letters appearing outside the alphabetical sequences stand out against the machine-tooled remainder. These additions include a MEDAL OF HONOR inscription.

There is a third carved Portland stone eagle to see, and it is the most stunning. For this you need to go downhill, making for the Cambridge Road entrance to the cemetery. The bald eagle here is quite different from the beast on the arms: the huge wings are stretched out straight, and it would be better to describe him as superbly bold.

The very large eagle in sunk relief was cut in situ.

MADINGLEY CHURCH

Outside to the south-west the Workshop designed a free, not mathematically rigid pattern for placing cremation stones. At the centre of the arc is a Portland stone (2003) REMEMBER BEFORE GOD. Individual stones are to fan out in radial fashion; so there is a Solnhofen light limestone for FRANK GRIFFITH DAWSON of 2008 to the left. The restoration of the church porch is commemorated by a 2010 Ancaster weatherbed stone in its floor (BROWN & WHITMORE).

Right: this is a long threshold across which visitors step into a formal garden. To ease walking over it, the letters are cut with the insides flat (as opposed to the usual v-cut). They are rough-pecked – the dirt settling there provides further contrast in time.

This is one of the cremation plaques that radiate from a central piece, in the arc of a circle. Initially the letters were painted green; when we added the widow's name, she asked for a more lively colour, in contrast to the green surround: brick-red.

MADINGLEY HALL

The handsome 16th century house is now a
centre for the Institute of Continuing Education
of the University of Cambridge. A garden of
exotic topiary on its north-west aspect has a long
2001 inscription on 6 slabs of Cumbrian green
slate in the ground. NO MAN CAN MAKE
A GREATER MISTAKE THAN HE WHO
DID NOTHING BECAUSE HE HIMSELF
COULD ONLY DO A LITTLE is the inspiring
message, and the author EDMUND BURKE
1729–1797 follows in italic capitals. David
Kindersley carved the University coat of arms in
situ over a doorway: head straight through the
main archway to the court beyond (1952).

With the account for 40 guineas, David Kindersley wrote
'I am sorry that the stone did not permit of greater detail,
but sometimes a limitation of this kind is not a bad thing'.
A corresponding (right) doorway shows his raw material
for the in situ carving.

61

Milton

A 1993 Welsh slate for the opening of the MILTON COUNTRY PARK is outside on the visitors' cafe. This park (south of the village) is home to an evocative large open green and tree plantation – head a few 100 yards directly east from the entrance. American WWII veterans often come here after their Madingley Cemetery visit. Because the central, triangular, 2 metre high pillar says THIS STONE COMMEMORATES THE 50TH ANNIVERSARY OF THE CESSATION OF HOSTILITIES IN EUROPE ON 8TH MAY 1945 AND THE FAR EAST ON 15TH AUGUST 1945. It is a 1995 Caen stone from Normandy, and stands in a hexagon of further 1995 inscriptions on York stone. They explain that the trees are for the 50th anniversary of the landing of the Allied Armies in France. And UTAH OMAHA GOLD JUNO SWORD are also there for those legendary Normandy beaches... stirring.

The opening slate is gilded and has some flourishes: the large L in particular has a flourish that fills the top space of the inscription, with two others for the middle on each side.

HIGH BRAVS SRV:O STIL 18th MAY FRE 1945

The powerful raised lettering wraps around this triangular pillar, from the top to the bottom.

This Church
was restored & beautified
for the Greater Glory of God
its vestry rebuilt, its organ renewed
and all blessed for worship
on Sunday 17 December 1972
by EDWARD LORD BISHOP OF ELY

GEORGE ROWLINSON, ERNEST DAY
CHURCHWARDENS
HERBERT FRANKLIN
RECTOR

Milton church is north of here, with an oval Welsh blue/black slate on the wall to the left of the altar: 'This Church was restored...' (1976).

Science Park
This site, north-east just outside the city border, is a remarkable Trinity College development begun in the 1960/70s; the college's long history of scientific prowess was ready ground for such an

HIS ROYAL HIGHNESS
THE PRINCE OF WALES
OPENED THIS BUILDING for
CAMBRIDGE CONSULTANTS
WEDNESDAY 1st AUGUST 1979

This is quite thick coloured glass in which the background has been blasted away, leaving the letters bold in clear glass.

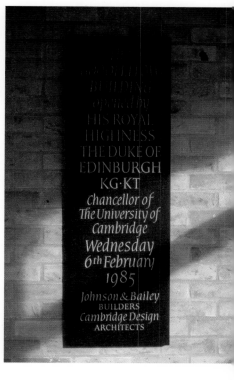

This stone
was unveiled by
the Chancellor of
The University of
Cambridge
HIS ROYAL
HIGHNESS
PRINCE PHILIP
DUKE OF
EDINBURGH
KG·KT
10th February 1986
The
CAMBRIDGE
INNOVATION
CENTRE
was built for
William Sindall &
and Christiania
Properties Ltd
to the design of
Biscoe & Stanton
by Sindall
Construction Ltd

GOODFELLOW
BUILDING
opened by
HIS ROYAL
HIGHNESS
THE DUKE OF
EDINBURGH
KG·KT
Chancellor of
The University of
Cambridge
Wednesday
6th February
1985
Johnson & Bailey
BUILDERS
Cambridge Design
ARCHITECTS

*adventurous throw. In keeping with the rapid turnover inherent
to scientific enterprise, the site has changed decade by decade. So
several inscriptions made for bygone years and occupiers are no
more. We illustrate the then opening glasses for CAMBRIDGE
CONSULTANTS (1979) and LASER-SCAN (1986); also
Welsh slates for the GOODFELLOW BUILDING (1985)*

this building was opened on Monday 10 February 1986 by
HIS ROYAL HIGHNESS PRINCE PHILIP DUKE OF EDINBURGH
Chancellor of the University of Cambridge

*On this glass (115 cm long) Lida engraved the letters by hand,
and then filled them with blue paint.*

ON THE
15TH OF JUNE 1989
HIS ROYAL HIGHNESS
THE DUKE OF EDINBURGH KG·KT
OPENED THIS BUILDING KNOWN AS
CAMBRIDGE INNOVATION CENTRE II
FOR
DENCORA PLC

and the CAMBRIDGE INNOVATION CENTRE (1986). Still to be seen are Welsh slates FOR DENCORA (1989), now Worldpay, and the KETTERINGHAM BUILDING (1991) at Cambridge Consultants. The FINNISTON AWARD of 1979 was a slate/glass 'trongle', i.e. 'the impossible triangle'.

David Kindersley loved flourishes – they cheer!

KETTERINGHAM
BUILDING
Dedicated to the memory
of
John Ketteringham
Director of Cambridge
Consultants
1981-1989

The triangle is an engineering feat, and floats in glass above the intricate letters cut in slate.

MORE'S MEADOW
Officially opened by
The Rt Hon Betty Boothroyd MP
Speaker of the House of Commons
9TH OF MARCH 1996

THE GREAT SHELFORD PAROCHIAL CHARITIES

Shelford

On the Cambridge Road approach to Great Shelford, two left turns at the railway bridge bring you into Bridge Close and More's Meadow; immediately on the left again you can see Betty Boothroyd's opening stone for
MORE'S MEADOW *(Welsh slate, 1996). Further into the village, beyond the bridge on this road, just before some stores on the left,* WILLIFIELD COTTAGES 32 *is a fine gilded 1991 Welsh slate outside 32 High Green.*

There is an art nouveau feel to the letter form flowing into the numerals.

In Great Shelford church a war memorial 'For remembrance and thanksgiving 1939–45' lists 20 names on a 1950 Welsh slate. It is fixed on the north wall, and moving in its quiet, unostentatious way. Outside in the churchyard (north again), a large group of cremation stones in the ground has 4 Welsh slates for *MARGERY HALE* (1996), *KATHLEEN FANNY BOORMAN* (1999), *JOHN BAYNTON ROLT* (2001)

Formal Roman capitals (bottom), less formal for italic capitals (middle), and all italics, with flourishes (top).

and *JOHN K. BYROM (2007).*

On to Little Shelford where the churchyard, some way down left of the church, has a tall 1981 headstone in Kirkstone green slate IN LOVING MEMORY OF THE CLAY FAMILY. The contrast between its stark appearance after 30 years' weather and the original workshop picture is striking.

The Workshop photograph documents the freshly cut stone – the times change and we change with them.

Stapleford

The cemetery is on the left down Mingle Lane, some distance before the church. There is a signposted approach track for vehicles. A riven Elterwater light green slate of 2009 for NEIL RAINE is near the rear of the cemetery, on the right of the central path. It is a jagged irregular rectangle; the one flat side edge is fine-rubbed for OUR LOVE HATH NO DECAY.

With an irregular piece obtained from the quarry, the drawing may not reflect the precise image for the finished work.

On the back is a formation of 4 stars: the fourth is the 'missing man', flying off into the unknown on his own – a motif both of aeronautics and life/death.

Wandlebury

The archway in Gog Magog House has a 1956/7 White Mansfield stone on the wall, commemorating the gift of this land by TERENCE GRAY.

Green slate riven is always a powerful rock. We have used its side as well as front and back for inscriptions.

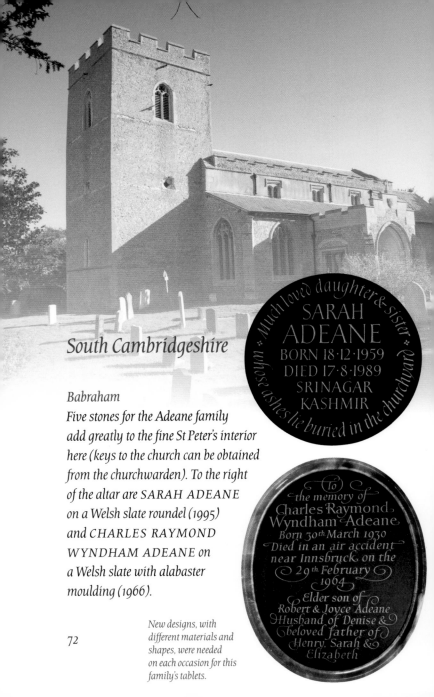

South Cambridgeshire

Babraham

Five stones for the Adeane family add greatly to the fine St Peter's interior here (keys to the church can be obtained from the churchwarden). To the right of the altar are SARAH ADEANE on a Welsh slate roundel (1995) and CHARLES RAYMOND WYNDHAM ADEANE on a Welsh slate with alabaster moulding (1966).

Much loved daughter & sister * whose ashes lie buried in the churchyard *

SARAH
ADEANE
BORN 18·12·1959
DIED 17·8·1989
SRINAGAR
KASHMIR

To
the memory of
Charles Raymond
Wyndham Adeane
Born 30th March 1930
Died in an air accident
near Innsbruck on the
29th February
1964
Elder son of
Robert & Joyce Adeane
Husband of Denise &
beloved father of
Henry, Sarah &
Elizabeth

New designs, with different materials and shapes, were needed on each occasion for this family's tablets.

THIS TABLET WHICH RECORDS THE
NAMES OF THE CHILDREN OF THOSE
COMMEMORATED ABOVE IS PLACED
IN THIS CHURCH OF THE BELOVED
HOME OF THEIR CHILDHOOD

Maud	1829·1853
Alethea m. Henry Grenfell	1829·1923
Robert	1830·1853
Lucy m. Admiral Sir Edward Sotheby	1831·1904
Henry m. Lady Elizabeth Yorke	1833·1869
Emmeline m. Reynd. Thomas Erskine	1835·1930
Edward m. Lady Edith Dalzell	1836·1902
Isabel m. Robert Smith	1839·1913
Mabel m. John Martineau	1840·1894
Jane	1842·1926
Constance m. Hugh Smith	1845·1918
Frederick	1847·1852

Below is a small 1967 Welsh slate for the grand JOHN PIPER window at the east. On the south wall of the nave a sumptuous Sicilian marble of 1961 records ...THE CHILDREN... of the family seen above.

The East Window designed
by John Piper, was given by
Sir Robert Adeane in memory
of his father and mother,
Charles and Madeline Adeane
July 1966

Balsham

For HANSLIP LONG OF BALSHAM and his wife MILDRED in the churchyard, see the Introduction under '1945 in Barton' (page 8).

Bartlow

At the rear of the church a Celtic cross of Portland Roach stone, made by other hands, has a quadrilateral 1956 Welsh slate on its base: in memory of JOHN VICTOR CHETWYND TALBOT.

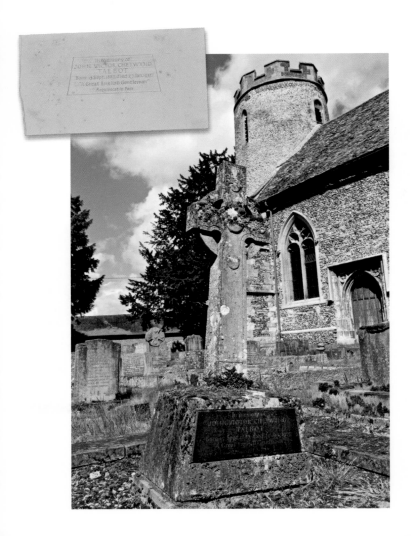

Fixing the Portland stone into position.

Bourn

The churchyard has a striking Portland stone of 2011 with a Celtic cross in sunk relief: JOHN JEREMY SEYMOUR MARSHALL. In Caxton End a T-shaped 1983 Kirkstone green slate BROOK COTTAGE (on approach to the house) is a playful interpretation of the brook.

Boxworth

A 2001 Welsh slate celebrates the restoration of CHURCH FARM, a particularly handsome house.

CHURCH FARM was restored by PETER FOSTER in 1972 for CHRISTOPHER & JOAN PARISH

Caxton
A headstone to the right in the churchyard is a 1991 Kirkstone green slate for FIONA MARY LATTIMORE.

Comberton
CHURCH FARM HOUSE (Clipsham stone, 1998), in Royston Lane north of the church, marks a beautiful building.

The flourish at the top echoes the traditional heraldic ribbons used for hanging the central lozenge (a lady's heraldic emblem as opposed to a gentleman's shield).

Cottenham

The church is north of the village; at the south-east fringe of the churchyard there is a headstone for MARTIN DOUBLEDAY (1993 Hopton Wood stone).

Elsworth

The Primary School has LTS on a 1998 Welsh slate in the entrance lobby. This stands for 'Loving Trusting Sharing', a past head's message for the school.

Eltisley

The churchyard in front of the church bears a 1991 Cumberland green slate headstone for DOROTHY JESSIE ALFORD.

Fen Drayton

The front of the churchyard has a ledger Welsh slate of 1993 in the ground for *DORIS TULIP*. To the left of the church there is *ANGELA RUSSELL BOYLE*, a headstone (Ketton stone 1989).

The village also had an Elterwater green slate for 'Riccardo Austoni An Italian gardener in England...' (1999).

Riccardo Austoni
An Italian gardener
in England
Nato 27 Dicembre 1938 Brescia
Morto 15 Dicembre 1998
Huntingdon
riposa in pace

The overall texture of this Ketton stone is dominated by the open capital letters, with little interlinear space – contrast with the *ALFORD* slate opposite.

Foxton

The churchyard in front of St Laurence's church, on the extreme left, has a 2004 blue-grey slate for DR KENNETH HUNTER... HERE LIES AN HONEST MAN. A smaller stone marks the foot of the grave: KH.

The totally rounded edges of both stones are hard work, but give a pleasantly soft feel.

DR KENNETH
HUNTER MA
1932-2002
SCHOLAR † TEACHER
HEADMASTER

HERE LIES AN HONEST MAN

Great Eversden
On the south-east fringe of the
churchyard a 2006 blue-grey slate
is a headstone for LUCY MARY le
BRETON BRIDGEWATER.

Great Wilbraham
St Michael's churchyard has
headstones of green slate for
MICHAEL DAVID ADAM
HANMER (2005), and for
RICHARD JULIAN BISIKER
(2008); sited on the south-east and
northern fringes respectively.

*The letters chosen for the headstone on the
right (BISIKER) derive from centuries of
differing traditions. Note for instance the
varying 'e': at first Greek on top, then Lombardic
(FATHER & ROSE), finally Roman (JANE).
There is also much nesting of letters into one
another. 'Love is eternal' has raised lettering
with the background pecked away.*

In proud
and loving memory of

MARY ELLISON

Born at Ealing 13 November 1864
Died at Cambridge 2 July 1953

The dearly loved mother of nine children

✝

A very great & courageous lady
& servant of Christ, who in a life-
time of loving kindness brought
comfort strength & gladness to
those around her & was beloved
& esteemed by all who knew her

R.I.P.

Blessed are the pure in heart
For they shall see God

Hadstock

The churchyard in front of St Botolph's is large, and in its north-east corner stands a 2007 Portland stone for BERYL MAY STEWART & DONALD RAE STEWART. The 'sun's ring of fire' on top derives from St Botolph's unique 14th century Finial Cross – it could be even earlier. There is a long history to this potent pre-Christian symbol.

This stone is set into the wall, bedded down on two Hopton Wood corbels, and with a generous border chiselled back to leave a raised panel.

The Finial Cross was deeply carved in relief.

BERYL MAY
STEWART
1931-2001
– Deeply loved by all –
&
heartfelt thanks

DONALD RAE
STEWART
1921-2009

Harlton

The church has a large 1954 Hopton Wood stone for MARY ELLISON on the north wall near the altar, chiming in with 3 other family memorials here. In the churchyard (south-east fringe) BRIAN CORRINGHAM GARFIT is a 1999 Welsh slate with crest and SEMPER IDEM on top. His wife JEAN HELENA was added in 2007.

The heraldry has been carved out of an oval set back into the stone, leaving the fine heraldic features standing proud.

SEMPER IDEM

In loving memory of
BRIAN CORRINGHAM
GARFIT
Born April 25th 1904
Died October 25th 1997
and his beloved wife
JEAN HELENA
Born September 1st 1913
Died December 13th 200

To cut in situ is lettercutters' delight: you smell the
air it's in, and can judge the environment precisely.

Harston

Harston House has an inscription (with dates) for GREENE
ARMSTRONG. They loved this place (2000). This was cut in situ: a
Ketton stone lintel on a beautiful house.

Hinxton

The Wellcome Trust's Genome Campus here began as the Sanger Centre
– simply 21st century biological science on high. That start is celebrated

by THIS PLAQUE
WAS UNVEILED BY
FRED SANGER, a 1993
Welsh slate in the Sulston
Building (the campus is not
open to the public).

84

The occasional ligature helps an even texture – here
UE, WA & UN in the first line, and HE twice in the
last two.

Linton

The oak WWI war memorial in St Mary the Virgin's
church is on the north wall of the nave. In 1959 David
Kindersley was asked to add 13 WWII names below;
the 1914–1918 dates were also moved then. Nearby is
THE SHRUBBERY in Mill Lane, a charming 1960
letterbox surround of Hopton Wood stone.

*WWII names
added skilfully
to make a new
whole, 14 years
behind time.*

*David Kindersley
moved to this
house in Linton
and carved his
own letterbox – so
of course there are
flourishes.*

85

Outside Linton to the north is CHILFORD HALL. Two Elterwater green slates mark the entrance drive; made in 1996, one had to be replaced following damage in 2009. In a private garden there is a massive 2003 Bath stone boulder for SAM ALPER, with a Hebrew inscription on the opposite side. It was carved in situ.

This is a place for entertainment and good cheer – the nameboards reflect this.

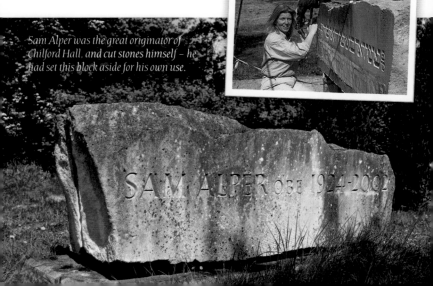

Sam Alper was the great originator of Chilford Hall, and cut stones himself – he had set this block aside for his own use.

SAM ALPER OBE 1924-2002

Lolworth
The All Saints churchyard
has a headstone to the
south, NINA NONA
DONADA ...finally
together with her beloved
CHARLES..., a Kirkby
blue-grey slate (2003).

Longstanton
To the left of the churchyard
entrance path there is
EVELYN-EVE-LOGAN,
a green slate headstone of
2005. Its back has 'Thine be
the Glory'.

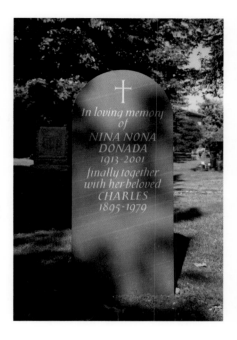

*This stone was
at the centre
of a 2005 BBC
documentary on
the Workshop.*

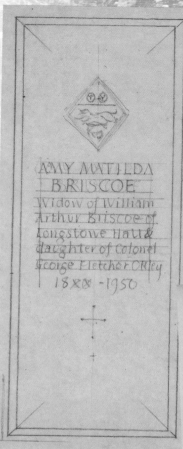

AMY MATILDA
BRISCOE
Widow of William
Arthur Briscoe of
Longstowe Hall &
daughter of Colonel
George Fletcher Oakley
1888 -1950

RICHARD GEORGE
BRISCOE M.C.
Son of
William Arthur
& Amy Matilda
Briscoe
1893-1957
Member of Parliament
for Cambridgeshire
and Lord Lieutenant
of the County

*This family were true patrons, with a
wealth of commissions. We begin with the
much weathered ledger stones in the
churchyard; the pieces that follow on the
next pages, inside the church, are still
more varied and colourful. The Hopton
Wood and marble memorials all have
fully raised, painted and gilded heraldry:
big stones that record remarkable lives.*

Longstowe

The church (keys from the churchwarden) and churchyard are a trove for fine stones commemorating members of the Wentworth Stanley family. The yard has three ledger stones immediately west of the church, for AMY MATILDA BRISCOE (Portland stone, 1951), RICHARD GEORGE BRISCOE (Portland stone, 1958) and AMY FLORENCE BEVAN (Forest of Dean stone, 1979). A large 1952 Welsh slate on a Portland stone base is also a ledger, at the north-west corner of the church: the long inscription is IN MEMORY OF THE CHILDREN OF... (Wentworth Stanley). A fifth ledger is a little way off under a tree on the north-west fringe: MICHAEL GUY MOLESWORTH BEVAN, who was Lord Lieutenant of the county; it is another Forest of Dean stone (1993).

AMY FLORENCE
BEVAN
wife of
Temple Percy
Molesworth Bevan
daughter of
William Arthur
Briscoe
of Longstowe Hall
1895–1978

Side view — — — — 36" — — —

MICHAEL
GUY
MOLESWORTH
BEVAN
OF
LONGSTOWE
HALL
1926–1992
LORD
LIEUTENANT
OF THE COUNTY
AND HIS WIFE
MARY
1926–XXXX

18"

IN MEMORY OF THE CHILDREN OF SIDNEY STANLEY AND HIS WIFE SARAH
SIR CHARLES WENTWORTH STANLEY D.L.J.P.M.A. 6 FEB.1860 - 31 MAR.1939
Lᵗ·COL. ALAN SIDNEY WENTWORTH STANLEY D.L.,J.P. 30 APR.1861-16 MAR.1945
ETHEL WENTWORTH STANLEY WATERFIELD. 2 MAY 1862 - 8 JUL.1936
CAPT. HERBERT FOSTER WENTWORTH STANLEY, 9ᵗʰLancers. 2 JUL.1863-28 APR.1900
ADA ELLEN WENTWORTH STANLEY BARTHROPP. 5 NOV.1864
GRACE WENTWORTH STANLEY STANLEY. 2 NOV.1865 - 23 JAN.1947
GUY WENTWORTH STANLEY. 21 JUL.1867 - 22 JAN.1949
JOHN CYRIL WENTWORTH STANLEY. 9 DEC.1868 - 7 NOV.1940
CONSTANCE EVA WENTWORTH STANLEY STANLEY. 4 JUL.1870 -12 JUL.1939
FLORENCE HOWARD WENTWORTH STANLEY STANLEY. 1 JUN.1872 - 27 AUG.1926
MAURICE WILLIAM WENTWORTH STANLEY. 21 JAN.1874 - 8 SEPT.1942
WINIFRED WENTWORTH STANLEY STANLEY. 19 JUN.1877
MARGUERITE SARA WENTWORTH STANLEY SENIOR. 26 MAR.1879 - 2 JAN.1947

Flat stones are called ledgers, and are subject to intensive weathering because of water accumulating.

There is also a cremation stone to the right of the church approach, a 1977 Welsh slate for JOHN EDWARD PERRY.

The Chandeliers
were given in memory of
Richard George Briscoe
1893-1957

Inside the church, pause
by the door, immediately
right, for a small 1974 Welsh
slate about the chandeliers
in memory of *RICHARD
GEORGE BRISCOE.*
At the west end an inscribed
stone corbel underneath a
small statue has *TEMPLE
PERCY MOLESWORTH
BEVAN (1983).*

The raised lettering wrapped
around this Portland stone
catches the light excitingly.

There is a grand finale to this visit at the northern transept, in a chamber for the Wentworth Stanleys. You face 6 inscribed stones, 5 of them from the Workshop, with heraldry to the fore. They commemorate a distinguished soldierly family that saw service in both world wars, and many evocative theatres of war are mentioned here. Beginning top left and working anti-clockwise, there is ALAN SIDNEY WENTWORTH STANLEY (Hopton Wood stone, 1952). Then SIDNEY NATHANIEL SHAFTO BARTHROP (Hopton Wood stone, 1952) and CHARLES SIDNEY BOWEN WENTWORTH STANLEY (Nabresina marble, 1972). We skip a stone to reach ALAN WROUGHTON WENTWORTH STANLEY (Nabresina marble, 1957) and HERBERT FOSTER WENTWORTH STANLEY (Hopton Wood stone, 1952). Beneath this array is a 1971 frieze of Nabresina marble, in three sections 3 metres long: central heraldry, and space for future family members.

Yes, this family were great patrons. Their heraldry is fully painted and gilded, and stands proud of the sunken panel (just like the borders). This planing down of the interior is hard work – compare page 120.

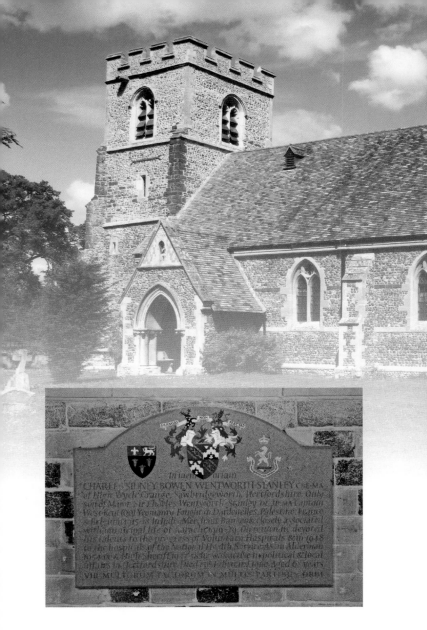

These memorials started off in the 1950s with an English limestone (Hopton Wood); this became difficult to obtain from the 1960s on, so Nabresina marble was then used. It is similar in looks.

93

Meldreth

The parish cemetery in Fenny Lane, near Whitecroft Road, is quite separate from the church. On the left of the path here (north-west quarter) stands a 1997 green slate REMEMBER FLORRIE & TOMMY MEIKLE.

The parents of Alec Meikle, who built the extensions to the Workshop.

Newton

In the churchyard WINIFRED ANNIE LUMBY is a 2004 green slate, west of the tower.

Over
*In St Mary's churchyard, at the rear, a
headstone for ANTHONY RONALD
TUBBS is a 2007 Portland stone.*
 *There is a striking house number '4' in
Whines Lane on a 2006 Welsh slate.*

*Mr Tubbs came to the Workshop in order to commission his
own gravestone, and was much involved in the design.*

In
memory of
ANTHONY
RONALD
TUBBS
11 Nov 1930
21 June 2006
husband of
KATHLEEN

*V-cut lettering changes its presence throughout the day – contrast the
two sides shot here at the same time, in and out of sunlight.*

Pampisford

*The eastern fringe of the churchyard has a remarkable Forest
of Dean stone: with two faces. The 1991 side is for CHARLES
ANTHONY HELLYER HODGE; in 2009 the other was
inscribed for his wife CYNTHIA HODGE.*

Papworth Everard
*Inside the Library, at Lower
Pendrill Court, a 2001 glass
plaque is on the wall for
the opening by the Duchess
of Gloucester.*

*Cambridgeshire has been active
in fostering new libraries, with
Kindersley glass for the opening.
The italics used here invite reading!*

96

Sawston

Sawston Village College began 80 years ago as the country's first community college. Henry Morris was the far-sighted founder, celebrated on a stone outside the Cambridgeshire County Council's offices on Castle Hill, Cambridge (see 'Cutting across Cambridge', Cambridge University Press 2011). A 1950 war memorial is to the left after the school entrance, under a covered way: a Welsh blue/black slate with Caen stone moulding. Morris's dictum was/is 'from the cradle to the grave – education'.

A very carefully thought through, classic design; with an outline pelican using the same v-cut as for lettering (see caption on page 124).

St Mary's churchyard has a 2008 Portland stone east of the church, *JAMES STRUTHERS*.

Shingay
MANOR FARM is on the main village road, marked by a 1998 Welsh slate.

Thriplow
On the north wall of the churchyard *KENNETH CHARTERIS TWIST* is a 1985 Welsh slate tablet.

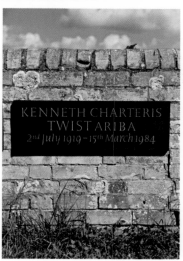

The name and dates in raised lettering, with a smooth surface and rough-pecked background, make a strong, factual beginning to this stone. Below, softer and quite different in layout, is the message of hope.

99

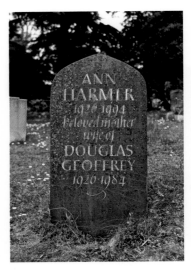

Toft
In the churchyard, to the south of St Andrew's, there is a 1996 headstone for ANNE HARMER of Elterwater green slate. Nearby a cremation plaque in the ground for WILLIAM NORGETT (Portland stone, 1999) bears symbols either side including spanner and compass: his engineer's tools.

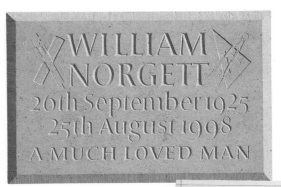

Weston Colville
The former workers' cottages of the d'Abo estate, west of the
road, have'd A 1966' cut into a Portland stone roundel set in the
pediment beneath the roof (1966).

The striking design in raised lettering was cut in
the Workshop, and fixed in position whilst high up
on scaffolding.

West Wratting
On the eastern fringe of the churchyard
*JOHN CATER & PAMELA CATER are
remembered on a 2010 green slate.*

*The flicks to letters and
numerals reflect the 'love
& joy' inscription.*

Whittlesford
A large ledger in the ground south-west of the church is a 1976
Portland stone for HAMILTON WILLIAM KERR.

Fixing stones on flint is a really difficult task.

TO THE MEMORY OF
CONSTANCE ELIZABETH
WIDOW OF THE REVᴰ JAMES ROBERTSON
HIS HELPER IN THIS PARISH 1891-1903
WITH RARE KINDNESS GAIETY AND MUSIC
LOVED & LOVING MOTHER OF SIX CHILDREN
BORN 6ᵀᴴ APRIL 1857 · DIED 26ᵀᴴ JANUARY 1935
ALSO OF HER TWO DAUGHTERS
WHO FOLLOWED THE WAY OF BOTH PARENTS
IN LIVES OF DEVOTED SERVICE TO OTHERS
SHEILA MARGARET
BORN 27ᵀᴴ APRIL 1881 · DIED 11ᵀᴴ DECEMBER 1945
GERDA CONSTANCE
BORN 22ᴺᴰ APRIL 1887 · DIED 28ᵀᴴ OCTOBER 1951

On the church itself, at eye-level on the wall of its eastern end, there is a Welsh slate of 1961 (actually designed 9 years earlier): a memorial tablet for CONSTANCE ELIZABETH ROBERTSON and two daughters SHEILA MARGARET & GERDA CONSTANCE.

Huntingdonshire

Brampton

On the eastern fringe of the churchyard there is a headstone for a noted neurologist: *FRANCIS M.R. WALSHE*, a 1974 Portland stone.

Buckden

REMEMBER FREDERICK FIELDING is a 1953 Welsh slate on the north wall inside the church, near the altar.

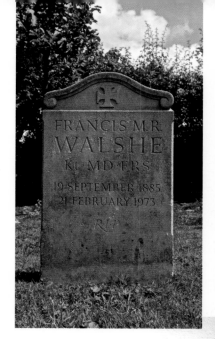

The top of this stone gives it a classic feel, looking back to the previous century when he was born

Remember Frederick Fielding M·B·E who died Oct. 18th 1948 aged 84 and his brother George who died July 18th 1949 aged 89. Benefactors of this Church and parish.

Bury

A stone for EVAN IDRIS EVANS is on the north wall of the church behind the rood screen (1957 Nabresina marble).

Diddington

In the church (south) there is a recess for the Thornhill family, with 6 earlier memorials; GEORGE EDMUND PETER THORNHILL was added in 2001, a Carrera marble mounted on a Welsh slate.

The rules of blazon (the method of specifying a heraldic device) allow plenty of room for artistic variation. The 6 preceding stones for this family lead up to ours, and illustrate that individual features may be altered over the centuries (like the lady on top). The original grant of arms is the rulebook – within it the artist can interpret.

... OF THE ELTON ESTATE
TO THE DESIGN OF
HOPE BAGENAL
MCMLVII

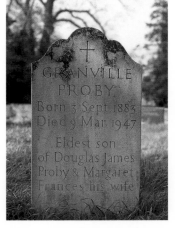

✝
GRANVILLE
PROBY
Born 3 Sept 1883
Died 9 Mar 1947

Eldest son
of Douglas James
Proby & Margaret
Frances his wife

Husband of ELISABETH ANGÉLIQUE Proby
JOCELYN
CAMPBELL
PATRICK
PROBY
1900·1993
Husband of KATHERINE

Elton
The churchyard has
3 stones for members
of the Proby family.
We show a headstone
for GRANVILLE PROBY
of 1950 in Ketton stone,
and a 1994/1997 Welsh
slate roundel in the
ground for JOCELYN
CAMPBELL PATRICK
PROBY. Both are on the
south-west fringe.

Elton Hall has been
the home of this family for
400 years; in the private
grounds there is a temple
with a 1958 Ketton stone
BUILT BY RICHARD
GEORGE PROBY.

Hemingford Grey

Two houses with Welsh slates on the outside: EIGHTEEN & HIGH STREET is from 2010, and TALLIS HOUSE from 2008 (at the river end of the same road).

The slate is square, and within it a triangle and circle: the 3 chief elements of design.

Hilton
The lych gate on the southern approach to the church is a WWI
memorial; in 1950 David Kindersley designed a bronze plaque,
on the left, to commemorate 3 WWII names.

Huntingdon
The Library in Princes Street had its 2009 opening by
EVELYN GLENNIE celebrated on a glass panel, seen in the
entrance porch.

Another library opening – hurrah!

NOKIA TELECOMMUNICATIONS · LANCASTER HOUSE ·

OPENED
BY
THE RIGHT HON
JOHN MAJOR
PRIME MINISTER
ON THE
24TH OF APRIL
1992

An occasion for gilded letters – and a round design for a global company.

In Lancaster Way there is the *NOKIA company and LANCASTER HOUSE – OPENED BY THE RIGHT HON JOHN MAJOR in 1992 – a Welsh slate roundel in the reception area.*

South-east, set by the river, All Saints Hartford has a fine 1950 Welsh slate, inside beneath the tower: another touching war memorial (see caption page 124). At Hinchingbrooke Park the opening of the Police Headquarters is marked by a 1973 Welsh slate, above the stairs in the entrance lobby. And in the same park site, the NHS Treatment Centre of Hinchingbrooke Hospital was opened by HRH THE PRINCESS ROYAL – a 2005 glass panel high up on the way in.

HIS ROYAL HIGHNESS
OPENED THIS BUILDING FOR THE MID-AN
CHAIRMAN ALDERMAN F.H. JEEPS M.C. VICE CHAIRMAN A
CHIEF CONSTABLE F DRAYTON PORTER OBE QPM ARCH

A long inscription of nearly 2½ metres.

The Chiming Set was installed in 1949 to the Glory of God & dedicated to the memory of Alfred George Ernest Jones & George William Arthur Mitchell and William Ernest Warren who lost their lives in the War of 1939-1945

After WWII there was a deep feeling for lost lives, and David Kindersley's war memorials capture it. See also the lych gate on the preceding page, and the reference to page 124.

E PRINCE OF WALES KG
OLICE AUTHORITY ON 30TH OCTOBER 1973
IAN LT-COL O N D SISMEY D.L CLERK W LIDDELL HANN
R ARTHUR CONTRACTOR R G CARTER (KINGS LYNN) LTD

Offord Cluny

The church is locked (keys with village shop); it has a recess (south) for the Sismey family. There were already 4 older marble memorials here – a challenge! So we have unashamedly derivative white marble stones for CATHERINE EDITH (1954) and GEORGE HERBERT SISMEY (1960), with PAULINE VINCENT (1981) in Sicilian marble, all on Welsh slate corbels as before.

112

For carving marble, exceptionally sharp tools are needed, so as not to bruise the stone.

IN MEMORY of
CATHERINE EDITH
WIFE of GEORGE HERBERT
SISMEY *Esquire* WHO DIED
ON THE 21ST MARCH 1953
AGED 78 YEARS

IN MEMORY of
GEORGE HERBERT
SISMEY *Esqr.*
formerly CHAIRMAN *of*
HUNTINGDONSHIRE
QUARTER SESSIONS
who died on
6TH JANUARY 1958
AGED 96 YEARS

IN MEMORY of
PAULINE VINCENT
WIFE of Lt-Col. OLIVER NORTH
DEANE SISMEY WHO DIED
ON 20TH SEPTEMBER 1980
AGED 68 YEARS

St Ives

THIS ALTAR WAS PLACED HERE... is in All Saints church, at the south-east corner of the nave: a 1966 Nabresina marble. Not far away, along Westwood Road, there is the One Leisure recreation centre; its entrance porch has a 1974 Welsh slate for the opening: DENIS HOWELL.

THIS RECREATION CENTRE
WAS OPENED BY
DENIS HOWELL M.P.
MINISTER OF STATE FOR
SPORT AND RECREATION
9TH SEPTEMBER 1974

The Egyptian hare was researched with care, and had to be turned round for the carving: in Western understanding forward movement is to the right, as in handwriting.

The addition of the husband to this stone is not by the Workshop.

ELIZABETH ANNE
MARIE GABRIELLE
THE HONOURABLE
LADY HASTINGS
Born 20 January 1934
Died 20 March 1997
AND HER HUSBAND
STEPHEN LEWIS
EDMONSTONE
HASTINGS KT. MC
Born 4 May 1921
Died 10 January 2005
Requiescant in pace

Peterborough & Fenland

Castor & Marholm
LADY HASTINGS is
the name here, a noted
Egyptologist as well as Deputy
Lieutenant of Cambridgeshire.
At Castor church there is AD
MAJOREM GLORIAM
DEI for her from 1998, a white
marble plaque with dove grey
marble border. It is set on the
south wall near the altar.

More meticulous Egyptology for the borders of these
marbles; we are fortunate in Cambridge, having
authorities at hand – e.g. the Fitzwilliam Museum
here. So note the friezes of ancient reed (above) and
lotus bud blossom (below).

In Marholm church this
AD MAJOREM inscription is repeated in the same materials – but
a 1998 marble of quite different shape and design. It is on the south
wall near the altar, close to a relief of Lady Hastings' grandmother. The
headstone for ELIZABETH ANNE...LADY HASTINGS is in the
south-west corner of the churchyard, a Mansfield white stone of 1998.
And the hare on the back: the Egyptologist liked this animal!

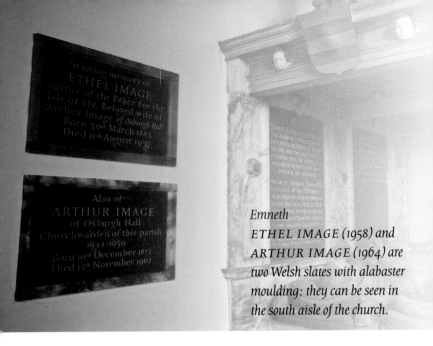

In loving memory of
ETHEL IMAGE
Justice of the Peace for the
Isle of Ely, Beloved wife of
Arthur Image of Oxburgh Hall
Born 30th March 1883
Died 11th August 1957

Also of
ARTHUR IMAGE
of Oxburgh Hall
Churchwarden of this parish
1944-1959
Born 10th December 1872
Died 15th November 1963

Emneth
ETHEL IMAGE (1958) and
ARTHUR IMAGE (1964) are
two Welsh slates with alabaster
moulding; they can be seen in
the south aisle of the church.

To the memory of
George Sharman J.P. 1845-1929
Churchwarden 1886,1890-1907
and his wife
Fanny Pope 1849-1933
their sons
George William 1873-1952
Churchwarden 1912-1918
Arthur Frank 1875-1961
Churchwarden 1908-1911
Herbert Percy 1876-1950
Algernon 1877-1975
Walter 1881-1961
and their daughter
Gertrude Fanny Sheppard
1885-1958
By the grace of God I am what I am

March
St Peter's church commemorates
GEORGE SHARMAN
and 7 family members on
a 1976 Welsh slate in the
south-west corner.

The opening of MARCH
LIBRARY is celebrated by a
2001 glass panel, to the right
after the entrance.

Yet another
library!

MARCH LIBRARY
opened by
His Royal Highness
The Duke of Gloucester
KG·GCVO
13th March 2001

Orton Waterville

*On the southern fringe of St Mary's churchyard there is a 1974
headstone for FRED BASON, in Kirkstone/Cumbrian green
slate. It has a book above and quill below for 'the best known of
all Cockney authors'; his diary was introduced and edited by
Noel Coward.*

*In a gravestone you try to reflect the life of the person
commemorated, hence all the ingredients to this slate.*

*Peterborough
The Cathedral of St
Peter first: the entrance
passage has oak panels
on each side. Left there
is HER MAJESTY
QUEEN ELIZABETH
DISTRIBUTED THE
ROYAL MAUNDY
(1977); two panels
sited right celebrate a
visit by the Queen and
Prince Philip for a 750th
anniversary (1989).*

*These panels were cut
and gilded in the
Workshop, and then
fixed. There is the same
height from the
beginning to the
ending of the lettering
in all 3, which made
the middle panel the
most challenging –
and lively!*

HER MAJESTY
QUEEN
ELIZABETH
DISTRIBUTED
THE ROYAL
MAUNDY
IN THIS
CATHEDRAL
27 MARCH
1975

HER MAJESTY
THE QUEEN
&
HIS ROYAL
HIGHNESS
THE DUKE
OF
EDINBURGH
VISITED THIS
CATHEDRAL

TO
COMMEMORATE
THE 750TH
ANNIVERSARY
OF THE
CONSECRATION
ON THE
20TH DAY
OF MAY
1988

In order to have the crozier in relief, the whole surface of the stone had to be planed down.

The window in this chapel is
dedicated to the memory of
SPENCER LEESON D.D.
Bishop of Peterborough
1949-1956
Born 9th October 1892
Died 27th January 1956
SHEPHERD   TEACHER   FRIEND

Then two chapels off
the South Transept
– the first for St
Benedict shows a 1958
Nabresina marble
stone on the left
*THIS WINDOW...
SPENCER LEESON.*
Next is St Kyneburgha's

with an inscription round the base of an Annunciation, *PRAY
FOR CLARE WIFE OF ALAN DURST (in a composition
material of 1977). At the east end beyond the altar is 'The New
Building' (from around 1500!), with two large benefactors' Welsh
slates on the left, THE DEAN & CHAPTER and MAJOR
DONORS (2002).*

*These slates were carefully designed to fit into the existing
stonework. The emblem on the right-hand one is derived from
the central west window of the cathedral.*

This Courthouse
was opened by
Her Majesty the Queen
22 March 1978

The inscription was done into 'engineering brick' which is very hard – sparks flew as we cut. The whole workshop was at it, toiling for several weeks, and wearing protective kit like goggles. The letters are formed by spaces cut into the brick; and they were then stained with dark, thinned-down paint.

The Magistrates' Court nearby 'was opened by Her Majesty the Queen', a 1978 Welsh slate behind the ushers' desk. This entrance hall also has a massive 1978 inscription hewn into the brickwork on the right 'Do right to all manner of people after the Laws and Usages of this Realm'; unhappily it is now largely obscured by a new lay-out.

The men are in alphabetical order, but their first names are given equal weight. They are individuals therefore. David Kindersley insisted on making his war memorials tender records of real people lost, not mere roll-calls.

In Woodston, south of the Nene, St Augustine's church has a 1956 Welsh slate on an inside wall at the south-west corner: a 1939–1945 war memorial with a roll-call of 23 names FOR REMEMBRANCE AND THANKSGIVING.

Further south of the river there is sheltered housing off Fletton High Street, at Fleetway/King's Road, with a 1985 Welsh blue/black slate naming MAUD SWIFT COURT.

For Remembrance and Thanksgiving
+
LEONARD BAKER
RONALD BEE
KENNETH CHURCH
GEORGE COCKER
JOHN DIXON
SIDNEY ELLENDER
SWANTE HILL
GEORGE HILLSON
WALTER HITCHBORN
CHARLES HOVELL
KENNETH JOHNSON
RONALD MARTIN
GEORGE ROGERS
ALEC SMITH
DOUGLAS SOWMAN
HEW TOMPSON
SIDNEY TINKLER
LESLIE TOOGOOD
VINCENT VENN
ARTHUR WARDLE
EZRA WARDLE
WILLIAM WEST
FRANK WOODWARD

1939-1945

MAUD Swift COURT

See page 64 for comparing different solutions in the same material.
Here the letters are blasted deep into the glass. The dots appearing in between are integral to the design – some also serve as fixing points.

HIS·ROYAL
E·DUKE·OF·C

And north to Thorpe Wood Police Station, where the opening BY
HIS ROYAL HIGHNESS THE DUKE OF GLOUCESTER
is marked by a 1980 bronzed glass panel, to the right in the
entrance hall.

Upwell
The church has a fine 1939–45 war memorial for 10 names
beginning with DOUGLAS GOOCH, a 1950 Welsh slate with
Portland cap and corbels; it is in the south aisle.

*Another characteristic
Kindersley war
memorial (see opposite
and pages 97 & 111).*

In memory of
CHARLIE
1972 - 2002
Ch. Gelding
by
PRINCE RHOY

Beloved for
his courage &
gentleness·

S·L·E·H

Wansford
A favourite horse is
remembered in the grounds of
Stibbington House on a 2003
Portland stone: CHARLIE...
Beloved for his courage &
gentleness.... The initals at the
bottom are for Stephen Lewis
Edmonstone Hastings.

CHARLIE
1972 - 2002
chestnut
Gelding by

Sir Stephen was
excited by fine
lettering – see
pages 114 & 115
for Castor &
Marholm.
So a commission
came for
celebrating the
horse he rode to
many victories.

In memory of
MARIAN ELIZABETH LEFEVRE
widow of Alderman John Lefevre who died
18th January 1926 & of their daughter
ELLEN ROSTOLL
widow of Robert Rostoll who died
23rd January 1953 by whose generosity
the bells of this Church were repaired
R · I · P ·

Whittlesey

St Mary's church in Station Road has a touching Welsh slate of 1957 for MARIAN ELIZABETH LEFEVRE and her daughter 'by whose generosity the bells... were repaired'.

Wisbech

The A1101 Freedom bridge ...WAS OPENED BY SIR HARRY LEGGE-BOURKE, a 1971 riven Westmorland green slate mounted at the south-east end. The Oasis Centre in St Michael's Avenue has a 2005 glass panel for the opening by HER ROYAL HIGHNESS THE PRINCESS ROYAL, in a hall to the right of the entrance.

This highly unusual bowed square of a slate is an experimental shape, mirroring a bridge's arch.

The Village Community and Children's Centre
opened on 16th November 2005 by
Her Royal Highness The Princess Royal

East Cambridgeshire

Bottisham (see also Lode)

In 1952 there were 3 commissions for the north-west chapel of the church by the Fairhavens of Anglesey Abbey. A Welsh slate inscription in front of the altar rail is 'in loving memory of Cara Leland Lady Fairhaven

(dates) the western chapels of this church were offered by her elder son Lord Fairhaven 1952'. The floor here bears a relief carving of the coat of arms (Welsh slate). The same heraldry appears over the chapel's last pew: a deep relief carving in Caen stone, painted and gilded.

Carving a coat of arms into the floor needs very deep relief; it is a tradition stretching over centuries.

*To cut these beasts with their horns, wings and tails
in the round – in stone! – is an amazing feat.*

ROGER SOAME JENYNS
Scholar Collector. Author and
Connoisseur of Far Eastern Art
Died 14ᵗʰ October 1976 aged 72 yrs
Much loved by his wife and two sons

David Kindersley also added two lines to
an existing tablet by the church's north
door in 1952.

On the north wall of the approach
to the main altar there is a 1978 Welsh
blue/black slate for *ROGER SOAME
JENYNS*. His headstone is in the
cemetery, a short walk north-east of the
church: a 1978 White Mansfield sand-
stone in the extreme north-east corner of
the site, where there is a separate plot for
that family.

*Two memorials to the same person, one inside the church, the other in
a graveyard: the thinking is completely different. A church memorial
is now most often a tablet on a wall (not a full-length burial stone as
before) – it has to be quiet and fit into its surroundings. A gravestone
has to stand out, on its own, in all weather.*

In 1996 a Turkish marble cremation stone was made for *VICTOR THOMAS MANNI*, intended for the churchyard.

Brinkley
A cremation stone to the left of the church entrance is for *ADA JULIA ALICE BLETCHER* (Welsh slate, 1991).

In the north-west corner of the churchyard stands a 2007 Welsh slate with 'Friendship, Compassion, Humour' on the back; for a much loved young man, *STEPHEN MACKLIN*.

Burrough Green
On the eastern side of the
southern exit from the village,
Bradley Road, a pair of
cottages have 1949 Ketton
stone relief work facing the
road. Centrally is '1948' in a
rectangle, and each house has
round heraldic designs with the initials R W & O G for Robert
Way and his wife Garett's arms.

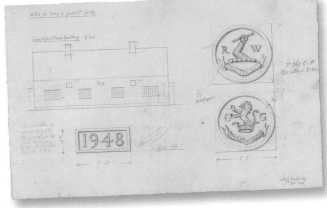

All 3 designs were used on these cottages.

In memory of
BASIL MacLEOD
BACON
who lies beneath
his favourite Beech in
Ash Wood, Chippenham
Beloved husband of
DOROTHY
Born 25th. October 1904
Died 24th. December 1958

Chippenham
Inside the church,
on the north wall,
a 1961 Welsh slate
commemorates
BASIL MacLEOD
BACON. Obliquely
opposite the church,
the entrance to THE
SCHOOL HOUSE
has a Welsh slate
roundel (1982).

The mantling thrown around the
helmet is a heraldic feature that
allows generous freedom in design;
David Kindersley was adept at this,
and exploited his love for flourishing.

Unusual: the reason we do not generally sign our work is that the lettering itself is our signature.

Dullingham
Inside the church on the north wall is IN MEMORY OF MARY MARIANNE MARIANA ROBINSON, *a 1947 Hopton Wood stone on two corbels. Very unusually, it is signed: D. K. 9. 7. 47.*

Haddenham
Inside Holy Trinity the east wall of the South Transept bears a large oval Welsh slate of 1984 for BENJAMIN GEORGE BURTON FOX, *soldier and vicar.*

134

✝
BENJAMIN
GEORGE BURTON
FOX M.C.,T.D.,
born 28th July 1912·died 6th Nov.1978
Chaplain H.M.Forces 1939-45
Vicar of St Andrews, Bedford 1946-50
Rector of St James, Montego Bay and
Archdeacon of Cornwall, Jamaica 1950-55
Vicar of St Etheldredas, Fulham 1956-65
Archdeacon of Wisbech
Vicar of Holy Trinity
Haddenham
1965-78
be thou faithful unto death & I will give thee a crown of life

The line of italics curving round the bottom looks like a necklace to the stone. Note that it begins with letters leaning backwards on the left, straightening in the centre, and then inclining forwards conventionally on the right.

Kennett

There has been much development/change on the large Lanwades site. A Welsh slate THIS FOUNDATION STONE WAS LAID BY LADY STANIER survives from 1966, but was for a Small Animals Research Centre no longer there; plans are to add the stone to a new complex here.

We make stones to outlast buildings.

Lode (see also Bottisham)

The dates hint that the Fairhavens of Anglesey Abbey shifted attention from their chapel at Bottisham in the 1950s to St James in the 1960s. Their new chapel in this church again has a floor inscription under the altar rail THIS CHAPEL WAS

BUILT 1960–1962 ... URBAN HANLON BROUGHTON AND CARA LELAND LADY FAIRHAVEN ... LORD FAIRHAVEN ... (1962 Welsh slate). The coat of arms is on another Welsh slate (1963) in the floor. And at the back there is more stunning carved heraldry (1966 Welsh slate) with a 1967 Welsh slate below, set in Sienna marble moulding: REMEMBER URBAN HUTTLESTON ROGERS BROUGHTON LORD FAIRHAVEN.

The marble moulding adds a dramatic touch to this memorial, and is a subtle link to the slate on the opposite page.

Behind the chapel there is a 1968 Portland stone on the east wall, for him AND CARA LELAND LADY FAIRHAVEN.

We cannot leave without visiting Anglesey Abbey. The house's new galleries (first floor) have a 1956 Welsh blue/black slate on a north-facing wall, with carved heraldry above. It records the 3 men who imagined, designed and built the galleries, headed by LORD FAIRHAVEN.

Compare the comment on the animals of page 129: to watch David at work, keeping the horns of the bull floating up unsupported, made everyone in the Workshop hold their breath at the time. This is all in slate, a layered material!

The base beneath a statue has to be subdued; but David Kindersley's extravagant spirit is in the inscription.

In the grounds (west) there is Temple Lawn with a statue of rock-slinging David; on its plinth 3 Welsh slate panels of 1954 show 2 JUNE 1953 and twice the F coronets. Lord Fairhaven wrote at the time 'Dear Mr Kindersley, I think they look extremely well...'; and they cost £25 each!

Mepal

You have to envisage a large airfield now obliterated by the A142 road; and go on to find a touching WWII memorial tucked away in the village at High Street/Laurel Close. This is a 1978 circular Kirkstone green slate on an octagonal Woodkirk brown stone plinth. It commemorates those who served here in No.75 NZ squadron, with its badge saying 'for ever and ever be strong'.

We like to fix our own stones and to see our work into its final position; here David Kindersley is putting the finishing touch to the task.

Snailwell
At the west end of the church, a blue-black Welsh slate of 1984
celebrates HENRY LONG WEBB, a churchwarden.

In memory of
HENRY LONG WEBB
beloved husband of Celia
for many years Churchwarden
Died 10 February in his 80th year
1903–1983

*A personal memorial in church adds both human interest and
historical context to the place.*

*Both designs here are in portrait format – the church decided on
landscape. There are two ways of fixing a stone. Permanent with
pins is our preferred method: the stone becomes part of the building's
fabric. Temporary (with a keyhole plate at the back for hanging) is
of course useful when shifts are a possibility.*

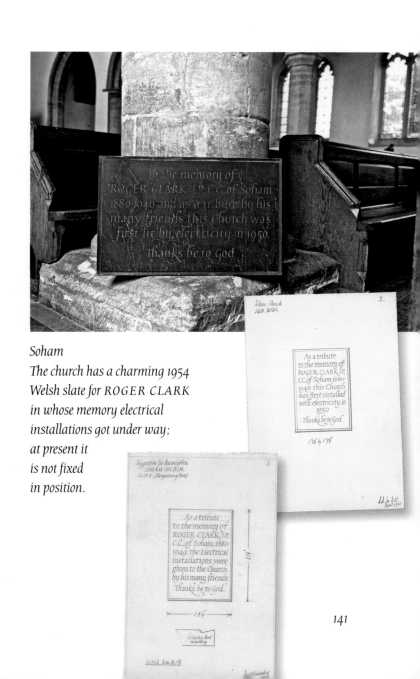

Soham

The church has a charming 1954
Welsh slate for ROGER CLARK
in whose memory electrical
installations got under way;
at present it
is not fixed
in position.

Soham Church.
Slate Tablet.

2.

As a tribute
to the memory of
ROGER. CLARK. J.P.
C.C. of Soham, 1880-
1940. this Church
was first installed
with electricity in
1950
Thanks be to God

12½ × 7¾

dd. for R.R.
April 1941

Suggestion for inscription.
SOHAM CHURCH.
SLATE (Abergavenny Blue)

1.

As a tribute
to the memory of
ROGER. CLARK. J.P.
C.C. of Soham, 1880-
1940. the Electrical
Installations were
given to the Church
by his many friends.
Thanks be to God

11½"

2¼'

fx testing flux'
installing

SCALE 2 in. to 1 ft.

141

Sutton
*The church tower with
its double octagon is
'unforgettable' (Pevsner),
and it watches over a large
burial ground. At the
extreme north-west fringe
there is a 2007 green slate
headstone for ALISON
MARY MAXEY.*

Swaffham Bulbeck
*Commercial End has a BAREFORDS
slate (2005) mounted as house sign.
At its north end the entrance drive to
the house opposite is marked by THE
ABBEY, a 1999 Barnack stone.*

*Barnack stone is no longer
quarried – but it is lovely to cut.*

Swaffham Prior
There is a newer churchyard
at the rear of the two churches,
across a track; a riven Welsh
slate on the left is for EDWIN
MUIR, POET (1958), with
a 1970 addition for his wife
and partner WILLA. It is of
unusual quadrilateral shape,
and the quotation are lines Muir
wrote about John Milton.

See the reference to this stone at the end of the Ely
Cathedral section (page 157).

Wicken

*In the village a 1975 oval Welsh slate marks THE MANGLE
HOUSE. At the National Trust's Wicken Fen site, the Visitors'
Centre shows a 1969 blue/black Welsh slate in the very centre
of the large floor area: a hexagon that simply and boldly
says '1969'.*

To set a date in a floor is a modest but effective way of marking an occasion.

The building of
these bungalows was first
suggested during the Episcopate
of Edward WYNN D.D. 1941-1956
& the land was bought
from his bequest

*'David Kindersley
in full flow' for this
lively inscription.*

Ely City

The Broad Street car park at the bottom of the
Cathedral hill is a frequent arrival site; a little way south before
this turning off Broad Street there is Wynn Close, gated. The
first pair of Clergy bungalows here bear a 1958 Welsh slate 'The
building of these bungalows... WYNN...'.

In the city centre, the Cloisters mall has
*ELY LIBRARY OPENED BY THE
BISHOP OF ELY*, a glass panel at the
top of the stairs (2000). Prior Crauden's
Chapel at The King's School is private
property; inscriptions cut into its altar
steps commemorate two headmasters,
JAMES KIRKLAND (1966) and
*BENJAMIN EDWARD NOBLE
FAWCETT (1970)*.

And another library!

IN MEMORIAM
BENJAMIN EDWARD NOBLE FAWCETT
1909–1969 HEADMASTER 1955–1969

Children do not have to be reminded of Mrs Needham every day, but might over time be tickled to find out what it all means: that was the thinking behind these startling letters.

Ely Community College in Downham Road is a large campus; there is a remarkable stone in the entrance porch of the Needham Tower building. It celebrates MRS CATHERINE NEEDHAM on a riven blue/black Welsh slate (1969). David Kindersley's angular letters make this an adventurous read, for the then County Council school.

Ely Cathedral
The untutored visitor could be forgiven for thinking about Elysium rather than eels when coming to this marvellous place. We begin beneath the fabulous Octagon where the south-east column bears a 2000 Welsh slate, well above eye-level: it celebrates 'the visit of HRH The Prince Philip … completion of the Cathedral restoration 1986–2000'.

*'Exuberant and yet restrained'
could be a Workshop motto – the
italics celebrate a great occasion.
Italics derive from the running
hand, which can be translated onto
slate, marking that joy.*

To the Glory
of God
This stone marks
the visit of
HRH The Prince Philip
Duke of Edinburgh
on 15 October 2000
to celebrate
completion of the
Cathedral restoration
1986-2000

On to the North Transept for 3 family stones on the west wall and floor: *HARRY LEGGE-BOURKE* is a 1973 Welsh slate with capping and sill of Portland stone; his wife *JEAN GRANT OF MONYMUSK* was added in 2008. In the floor beneath are Welsh slate diamonds for *EAH L-B (1973)* and *CJ L-B (2008)*.

Another example of David Kindersley's skill in design. That the best works can only be cast as they are, and not succeed in any other way, is a familiar theme in all art – he brought it to 20th century lettering.

*Obliquely opposite is St George's Chapel with a floor slab at the
entrance for MUIRHEAD COLLINS CLAYTON (1959 Welsh
slate recut in 1991).*

THIS
PROCESSIONAL WAY
STANDS ON
THE FOUNDATIONS
OF THE
LADY CHAPEL PASSAGE
USED BY THE
PILGRIMS TO ELY

BENEATH THIS FLOOR
LIE THE
MORTAL REMAINS
OF 27 PERSONS FROM
THE WIDER MONASTIC
COMMUNITY
REINTERRED DURING
BUILDING WORK

AD 2000

Off the North Choir aisle, the passage to the Lady Chapel shows two large and striking 2001 Ancaster stones in the floor: *THIS PROCESSIONAL ROUTE ... and BENEATH THIS FLOOR ....* In the Lady Chapel itself, a further floor slab is to the left in front of the altar; a 1974 Welsh slate for a distinguished soldier and bishop, *NOEL BARING HUDSON.*

Returning to the North Choir aisle and heading east, 3 tablets appear on the north wall. *HORACE MacCARTIE EYRE PRICE* is a 1974 Solstone; *GORDON JOHN WALSH* of 1976,

The lettering is very elongated because it will always be seen foreshortened. Solving the optical demands of large floor inscriptions is further illustrated by a massive piece in St Albans Cathedral (see the book Lasting Letters, Cambridge, Cardozo Kindersley Editions, 1992).

Since cutting Japanese letters is not straightforward, it is necessary to have Cambridge as a research resource.

HAROLD EDWARD
WYNN D.D.
BISHOP OF ELY
1941 - 1956

Fellow of Pembroke College
Cambridge

Born 1889 · Died 1956

He fed them with a faithful
and true heart

*Gold on heraldry adds
a rich sparkle.*

HAROLD EDWARD
WYNN
1889-1956
BISHOP OF ELY

*and HAROLD
EDWARD WYNN
of 1958 are both
Portland stones.*

*We have already seen this Bishop WYNN on the Clergy
bungalows in Ely City above; further east along the aisle his
name recurs on a floor slab in Bishop Alcock's Chapel,
a 1957 Welsh slate to the right of the altar.*

*The design is of
course inspired by
the floor mosaic.*

Crossing the Cathedral obliquely from here to the south, the Presbytery behind the Choir has a huge 1969 Welsh slate diamond in the floor: HERE STOOD THE SHRINE OF ETHELDREDA ....

HERE
STOOD
THE SHRINE OF
ETHELDREDA
SAINT AND QUEEN
WHO FOUNDED
THIS HOUSE
A.D
673

Thank goodness times are changing with regard to women's place in church memorials – it still took a long time for the wife to be accorded her stone.

IN MEMORIAM
JOHN MARTIN CREED D.D.,F.B.A.
FELLOW OF St JOHN'S COLLEGE
ELY PROFESSOR OF DIVINITY IN
THE UNIVERSITY OF CAMBRIDGE &
CANON OF THIS CATHEDRAL CHURCH
Born 14th October 1889, died 17th February 1940
Justorum animae in Dei manu sunt

In memoriam
MAY GERALDINE
1898-1959
wife of
JOHN MARTIN
CREED

And on into the South Choir aisle for two Portland stone tablets on the south wall, IN MEMORIAM JOHN MARTIN CREED (1955) and below MAY GERALDINE CREED (1979). We are moving into the South Transept and its St Dunstan's Chapel; left of the altar is a 1963 Hopton Wood stone slab for WILL SPENS Steward to the Chapter.

The floor of a church is now a great unexplored area, said David Kindersley. In the 21st century people tend to look up; once they expected only full-length burial stones as floor features. The appeal and modest size of this fine piece, and that on the opposite page, point a new way ahead – look down!

Finally and aptly: a floor slab for a stone man of renown. At the very western end of the Nave's south aisle, just behind the reception area, there is a 1977 Ancaster 'weatherbed' stone for DONOVAN PURCELL Surveyor to the Fabric. John Milton has 'fabric of the Heavens ... Orb in Orb' in Paradise Lost; we end with the lines inscribed on Edwin Muir's headstone at Swaffham Prior for Milton ' – his unblinded eyes saw far and near the fields of Paradise'.

The Keatley Collection

1952	BBC coat of arms	Welsh slate	33 × 48
1969	Alphabet	Welsh slate diamond	31 × 31
1969	Alphabet (capitals, italics, numerals)	Welsh slate (Birmingham)	53 × 30
1971	TRUTH IS SIMPLE...alphabet	Welsh blue-black slate (Birmingham)	20 × 20 × 6
1977	REFECIT MCMLXXV	Welsh slate roundel (Royston)	46 × 46
1977	Alphabet (italic)	Glass disc	25
1979	HENRY ANDREWS	Welsh blue-black slate roundel (Royston)	51 × 51
1980	1891 SD	Welsh slate (Royston)	47 × 45
1981	KILN HOUSE	Welsh slate (Royston)	47 × 37 1/2
1981	THIS HOUSE...HIRSCH	Welsh slate	37 × 47
1981	ROYSTON NATIONAL SCHOOL	Welsh slate (Royston)	70 × 85
1981	Because there is a word for it...	Glass bowl inscription	31
1983	CONGREGATIONAL SCHOOLROOM	Welsh slate (Royston)	70 × 74
1983	Alphabet (flourished)	a. Welsh slate b. Glass roundel	42 × 30 1/2 25 1/2
1984	SPARE NOT BUT WASTE NOT	Welsh slate oval	29 × 33
1986	Alphabet (flourished IJK centrally)	Welsh slate oval	53 × 66
1986	ABSTINVI LIBRIS IVVENIS	Welsh slate	17 × 102
1988	ARABELLA HELEN STRUTT...	Cecil Jordan wooden bowl inscription	47
1989	ROYSTON CORN EXCHANGE	Welsh slate triangle (Royston)	65 × 245
1990	Alphabet (wild calligraphic)	Welsh slate	33 1/2 × 30 1/2

1990	TEY HOUSE	Welsh slate (Royston)	74 × 55
1992	THE KEATLEY TRUST COLLECTION	Welsh slate	47 × 70
1998	IN GRATEFUL MEMORY OF...	Welsh slate roundel (London, Lansdowne Club)	64 × 64
1998	WHEELWRIGHTS 1997	Welsh slate roundel (Royston)	127 × 127
1999	1997	Welsh slate square (Easton near Huntingdon)	38 × 38
1999	MCMXCVIII	Welsh slate square (Saffron Walden)	61 × 61
1999	LAKE HOUSE	Welsh slate diamond	64 × 36
1999	IN MEMORY OF JAMES WALTER KEATLEY...AND OF HIS WIFE...	Portland stone	57 × 58
1999	Arthur Baker alphabet	Welsh slate	46 × 61
2001	ЯK	Alabaster box inscription	6 × 15 × 10
2006	Puzzle slate	Welsh slate roundel	25 × 25
2009	MOVE A STONE STIR A WING	Welsh slate ellipse	24 × 26
2009	The labour we delight in physics...	Welsh slate	56 × 46
2011	CHOP YOUR OWN WOOD...	Welsh slate	27 × 61

Churchyards & burial grounds

Balsham *(p.73)*

HANSLIP LONG OF BALSHAM & his wife MILDRED	1945	Portland stone

Bartlow *(p.74)*

JOHN VICTOR CHETWYND TALBOT	1956	Welsh slate

Barton *(p.28)*

IDA EDWARDS & HAROLD EDWARDS	2001	Welsh slate

Barton woodland burial place *(p.37)*

NICHOLAS THEODORE VENIZELOS TAPTIKLIS	2007	Oak bench

Bourn *(p.75)*

JOHN JEREMY SEYMOUR MARSHALL	2011	Portland stone

Bottisham *(p.128)*

Churchyard

VICTOR THOMAS MANNI	1996	Turkish marble

Cemetery

ROGER SOAME JENYNS	1978	Mansfield white sandstone

Brampton (p.105)

FRANCIS M.R. WALSHE	1974	Portland stone

Brinkley (p.131)

ADA JULIA ALICE BLETCHER	1991	Welsh slate
STEPHEN MACKLIN	2007	Welsh slate

Caxton (p.77)

FIONA MARY LATTIMORE	1991	Kirkstone green slate

Coton (p.39)

RITA HOWARD	2007	Green slate
DONALD ARTHUR PRATER & PATRICIA PRATER	2003/2005	Portland stone

Cottenham (p.78)

MARTIN DOUBLEDAY	1993	Hopton Wood stone

Eltisley (p.78)

DOROTHY JESSIE ALFORD	1991	Cumberland green slate

Elton (p.107)

ALICIA MARIA MURRAY	1950	Ketton stone
GRANVILLE PROBY	1950	Ketton stone
JOCELYN CAMPBELL PATRICK PROBY	1994/1997	Welsh slate

Fen Drayton (p.79)

ANGELA RUSSELL BOYLE	1989	Ketton stone
DORIS TULIP	1993	Welsh slate

Fen Ditton (p.40)

PETER ARUNDEL JEWELL	1999	Portland stone
ALFRED WATERS	1990	Kirkstone green slate

Foxton (p.80)

KENNETH HUNTER	2004	Blue-grey slate

Fulbourn (p.40)

Churchyard

ROSEMARY CAROLYN TOWNLEY	2004	Green slate

Cemetery

NORA FLORENCE SALT wife of ERIC DOUGLAS SYDNEY SALT	2010	Brown York stone
WINDSOR IAN WEBSTER	1994	Welsh slate

Girton (p.44)

JEAN BUITER	2006	Welsh slate
DAVID BERNARD EVANS	1998	Welsh slate
JOANNA MARY HARTLEY	1999	Welsh slate
MARGARET ROBSON	2004	Portland stone

at the City Crematorium (A14)

JUDITH MARIA LAUTERPACHT	1971	Bronze plaque on tree

Grantchester (p.47)

Pelican column (Corpus Christi College Fellows' Memorial)	1950	Portland stone
REMEMBER BEFORE GOD THE SOULS OF THOSE WHOSE ASHES...	1975	Welsh slate with Portland stone capping
GEORGE SIDNEY ROBERTS KITSON CLARK	1977	Ketton stone
GSRKC	1977	Portland stone
DENNIS NELIGAN COLE	2011	Portland stone
JOAN ELSA DAY	2005	Ancaster stone
LOUIS CAMILLE DE GLEHN and his wife MARION CASELS	1952 1975	Hopton Wood stone
MARY GERALDINE DICKINS	1977	Portland stone
PHILIP BASIL EMPEDOCLES	1976	Welsh slate with York stone paving
IRVING BAMDAS FRITZ	1999	Elterwater green slate
CHARLES BURFORD GOODHART	2001	Green slate
EDWYN CLEMENT HOSKYNS	1996	Additional name on Welsh slate
MICHAEL McCRUM	2006	Green slate
JOHN PENNINGTON	1977	Mansfield white sandstone
SHEILA ANNE RODWELL	2010	Portland stone
WYNIFRED MARY WALKER	1977	Additional name on existing stone

Great Eversden (p.81)

LUCY MARY le BRETON BRIDGEWATER	2006	Blue-grey slate

Great Shelford (p.67)

KATHLEEN FANNY BOORMAN	1999	Welsh slate
JOHN K. BYROM	2007	Slate
MARGERY HALE	1996	Welsh slate
JOHN BAYNTON ROLT	2001	Welsh slate

Great Wilbraham (p.81)

RICHARD JULIAN BISIKER	2008	Green slate
MICHAEL DAVID ADAM HANMER	2005	Green slate

Hadstock (p.82)

BERYL MAY STEWART & DONALD RAE STEWART	2007	Portland stone

Harlton (p.83)

BRIAN CORRINGHAM GARFIT & his beloved wife JEAN HELENA	1999/2007	Welsh slate

Histon (p.52)

Churchyard		
JAMES LUKE MACAULAY	2000	Portland stone
Cemetery		
STEPHEN OSWALD CHIVERS, & his wife MARJORIE EDITH & their daughter ELIZABETH ANNE	1995	York stone
WILLIAM NOEL CHIVERS	2002	Green slate

Little Shelford (p.69)

CLAY FAMILY (4 names)	1981	Kirkstone green slate

Lode (p.135)

URBAN HANLON BROUGHTON and CARA LELAND LADY FAIRHAVEN	1968	Portland stone

Lolworth (p.87)

NINA NONA DONADA with her beloved CHARLES	2003	Kirkby blue-grey slate

Longstanton (p.87)

EVELYN-EVE-LOGAN	2005	Green slate

Longstowe (p.89)

AMY FLORENCE BEVAN	1979	Forest of Dean stone
MICHAEL GUY MOLESWORTH BEVAN	1993	Forest of Dean stone
AMY MATILDA BRISCOE	1951	Portland stone
RICHARD GEORGE BRISCOE	1958	Portland stone
JOHN EDWARD PERRY	1977	Welsh slate
IN MEMORY OF THE CHILDREN OF... (Wentworth Stanley)	1952	Welsh slate on Portland stone base

Madingley (p.60)

REMEMBER BEFORE GOD THOSE WHOSE ASHES ARE BURIED HERE	2003	Portland stone
FRANK GRIFFITH DAWSON	2008/2011	Solnhofen light limestone

Marholm (p.115)

ELIZABETH ANNE MARIE GABRIELLE THE HON... LADY HASTINGS	1998	Mansfield white stone

Meldreth (p.94)

FLORRIE & TOMMY MEIKLE	1997	Green slate

Newton (p.94)

WINIFRED ANNIE LUMBY	2004	Green slate

Orton Waterville (p.117)

FRED BASON	1974	Kirkstone/Cumbrian green slate

Over (p.95)

ANTHONY RONALD TUBBS	2007	Portland stone

Pampisford (p.96)

CHARLES ANTHONY HELLYER HODGE CYNTHIA HODGE (on other side)	1991/2009	Forest of Dean stone

St Mark's, near Barton (p.28)

SETH DONALDSON	2000	Welsh slate
MILA GERSHEVITCH	1977	Horton stone
BARRY SLOAN MACKAY PRIEST	1967	Ancaster stone
CHRISTINE MARY BERTIE MACKAY	1965	Ancaster stone
RICHARD HOOK RICHENS and his wife RUTH HAMILTON SCOTT	1985/2003	Cumbrian Green slate

Sawston (p.97)

| JAMES STRUTHERS | 2008 | Portland stone |

Stapleford (p.71)

| NEIL RAINE | 2009 | Elterwater green slate |

Sutton (p.142)

| ALISON MARY MAXEY | 2007 | Green slate |

Swaffham Prior (p.143)

| EDWIN MUIR
& his wife and partner WILLA | 1958/1970 | Riven Welsh slate |

Thriplow (p.99)

| KENNETH CHARTERIS TWIST | 1985 | Welsh slate |

Toft (p.100)

| ANN HARMER
wife of DOUGLAS GEOFFREY | 1996 | Elterwater green slate |
| WILLIAM NORGETT | 1999 | Portland stone |

West Wratting (p.102)

| JOHN CATER & PAMELA CATER | 2010 | Green slate |

Whittlesford (p.103)

| HAMILTON WILLIAM KERR | 1976 | Portland stone |
| CONSTANCE ELIZABETH ROBERTSON
& SHEILA MARGARET
& GERDA CONSTANCE | 1961 | Welsh slate |